THE SOURCE OF LIFE

CHRISTOPH CARDINAL SCHÖNBORN

THE SOURCE
OF LIFE

Exploring the Mystery of the Eucharist

Edited by Hubert Philipp Weber

Translated by Brian McNeil

IGNATIUS PRESS   SAN FRANCISCO

Original German edition
Wovon wir leben können: Das Geheimnis der Eucharistie
Edited by Hubert Philipp Weber
© 2005 by Verlag Herder GmbH, Freiburg im Breisgau, Germany

English language edition
© 2007 by The Crossroad Publishing Company, New York, NY
All rights reserved

Biblical translations are taken from the Revised Standard Version
© 1973 by the Division of Christian Education of the National
Council of the Churches of Christ in the United States of America.

Cover art:
The Tree of Life and Last Supper
Taddeo Gaddi (c. 1300–1366)
Fresco. Former Refectory.
Museo dell'Opera, S. Croce
Florence, Italy
Photograph: Raffaello Bencini
© Alinari/Art Resource, New York

Cover design by Roxanne Mei Lum

Published 2013 by Ignatius Press, San Francisco
By arrangement with The Crossroad Publishing Company
ISBN 978-1-58617-784-3
Library of Congress catalogue number 2013930748
Printed in the United States of America ∞

CONTENTS

FOREWORD BY ONE WHO
HEARD THESE TALKS

From the very first days of the Church, the Eucharist has been supremely important—in a certain sense, it is the sign by which Christians are known, for as we read in the Acts of the Apostles about the life of the earliest community, "They broke bread in their homes" (2:46).

On the feast of Corpus Christi in 2004, Blessed John Paul II declared the period from October 2004 to October 2005 the Year of the Eucharist. The encyclical *Ecclesia de Eucharistia*, which the Pope published on Holy Thursday 2003, and this Year of the Eucharist offered a good opportunity to look anew at the central mystery from which we draw life. The present book has its origin in the catechetical talks held by Christoph Cardinal Schönborn, arch bishop of Vienna, in Saint Stephen's Cathedral. The shared reflection is carried out in the form of catechesis. This is not an academic lecture; rather, catechesis grows out of the faith and the action of the Church and is meant in turn to have an influence on this faith. The essential aim of catechesis is to strengthen the faith.

What do we mean when we say "the mystery of faith"? What helps to strengthen the faith? The first thing we must do is to look at what the Church does. How are we to understand the celebration of the Eucharist? Here it is helpful to look at the roots, especially the testimony of scripture and tradition—the celebration in the early Church, texts of the Church Fathers and theologians, or the teaching of the Church as this is summarized, for example, in the *Cat-echism of the Catholic Church.*

Three great themes are discussed in the ten chapters of this book. First, Cardinal Schönborn looks at the celebration of the Eucharist itself. The first chapter examines the Jewish roots of our liturgy, with particular emphasis on the Jewish prayers of praise and thanksgiving.

The celebration of Mass cannot be understood without the Passover celebration of the old covenant. Jesus too celebrated the Passover meal with his disciples, and many elements of this can still be found today in our liturgy. The second chapter takes up the question how Jesus celebrated the Last Supper.

The new element in the Last Supper is the words of Jesus: "This is my body; this is my blood." In the third chapter, the Cardinal looks at their meaning and asks: How are these words to be understood, symbolically or really?

The Church's reply has always been unambiguous. Jesus Christ is truly present for us in the eucharistic gifts with his Body and Blood. This is the mystery of the Eucharist, the second great theme in this book. Four key words play a central role in helping us to understand aright this meal to which Jesus invites us: *memorial, sacrifice, consecration,* and *presence.*

The subject of the fourth chapter is the directive of Jesus, "Do this in memory of me!" Here, the memorial means much more than merely thinking back to particular occurrences. One who remembers shares personally in the great event.

The fifth chapter takes up a concept that many people today find hard to understand: the Mass is a sacrificial meal. What meaning can a sacrifice have? If God is kind and loving, why then does the Bible say that sacrifices are to be offered?

The sixth chapter then asks what the transformation of bread and wine into the Body and Blood of Christ means.

The Eastern and the Western traditions have each reflected in a special way on one particular aspect of this event. The Cardinal presents these before looking briefly over the shoulder of Saint Thomas Aquinas as he sits at his writing desk.

The seventh catechesis discusses the concept of presence. What does it mean to say that the Lord is genuinely, truly, really present in the sacrament of the Eucharist?

The final great theme is the reception of Communion.

The eighth chapter speaks of the correct preparation for receiving the sacrament. It is a tremendous gift that we as Christians are allowed to share table fellowship with Jesus. What must we ourselves bring to the feast? How can we prepare ourselves?

The ninth chapter concentrates on eucharistic fellowship and its boundaries, which often cause people pain today, with reference to the situation of those who are divorced and remarried.

In the final chapter, ecumenical questions are discussed. The shared Eucharist is the goal of all our ecumenical endeavors, but it presupposes unity in the faith. How are we to conduct ourselves today in this regard? Is it possible for Christians of other confessions to receive Communion in the Catholic Church?

In order to shed light on the mystery of the Eucharist, Cardinal Schönborn presents and interprets examples from the Christian experience of life and examines the contribution made by theological thinking and argument to the defense of the Church's teaching before the tribunal of human reason. Reflection on the faith—including the examination of critical questions—and a deeper knowledge can strengthen our faith.

The editor

I

WHERE DOES THE MASS COME FROM?

"The Church draws her life from the Eucharist." These are the first words of the encyclical *Ecclesia de Eucharistia* of Pope John Paul II.

> The Church draws her life from the Eucharist. This truth does not simply express a daily experience of faith, but recapitulates *the heart of the mystery of the Church.*[1]

The Eucharist is the center of the Church's life and is her nourishment. This book is about this mystery that Christ has given to his Church.

A Precious Treasure in Earthen Vessels

A permanent deacon, Franz Eckert, relates the following experience.

> A young lady welcomed me at the airport of the Chinese capital and presented herself as the person who would accompany me. She was an academic translator, and her English seemed virtually without accent (as far as that is possible in

---

[1] *Ecclesia de Eucharistia* 1; italics in original. All quotations from Church documents are from the Holy See website, www.vatican.va, unless otherwise noted.

China). Her costume, which resembled a uniform, and her restrained politeness made her appear somewhat frozen. During the trip to the hotel, she offered to take me on a short tour of the city before the evening meal. The twilight of the Sunday afternoon was falling, and the air was heavy with snow clouds. What I wanted was not sightseeing but a Catholic evening Mass, and I told her this. After she had a brief consultation with the driver and made some calls on her mobile phone, the car brought us to a brightly lit church. Many people, most of them young, were streaming into the building. My companion told me that the Mass was in Chinese and that I would not understand anything. "The rite is the same everywhere in the world", I replied, and I got out of the vehicle. She wanted to stay in the car, but I told her, "You have been appointed to accompany me, and now you will attend the Mass with me." She came with me; only the driver remained in the car.

I went into the sacristy and saw a picture of our Lady and a photograph of the Holy Father—so I knew that I was in the right place. The priest did not speak English and I did not speak Chinese, but I showed him my stole. He embraced me and gave me an alb, and we celebrated the Mass together. Many people came to Communion, including numerous catechumens who asked for a blessing. The Mass was a dignified and joyful service.

When we left the church, my companion looked rather less frozen. She began to ask questions, although she apologized each time she spoke. "Is that God who comes to you there?" "Yes, it is God." "Is God in the golden vessels that you lift up at the altar in there?" "Yes, he is in the vessels, not symbolically but really. The priest changes bread and wine into the Flesh and Blood of our Lord." After a lengthy silence, she asked another question, this time apologizing twice. "And you . . . eat that?" "Yes, we eat it. If perfection exists anywhere on earth, that is the most perfect union between human beings and God. And the same thing happens wherever there is a Catholic priest, every single minute throughout the whole world." Once again, she fell silent.

It was only when we reached the hotel that she asked her final question. "How do you live with this religion?" I had no time to answer, because we had now entered the noisy reception area of the hotel; but one week later, she accompanied me to the airport, and when she bid me farewell before the passport control, she said, "Please write to me and send me something that I can read about this God." I promised to do so, and then I went through the barrier. I soon lost sight of her in the crowd. As I took my seat in the plane, I was filled with joy at this faith that permits us to give such answers to questions like that. And I thought of her final question, to which I did not reply—only life itself and the grace of God can answer it. We flew over Mongolia, and the country, covered with snow and lit up by the moon, spread out below us. "A precious treasure in earthen vessels", I thought, and I fell asleep.

"A precious treasure in earthen vessels." I wish to reflect on both of these, the treasure itself, the "mystery of faith", and the vessel that contains it, the liturgy. Where does the celebration of the Eucharist come from? How did it develop? What does it mean? Our first chapter will look at the origins of the Mass.

The Mass, the Eucharist, is "typically" Christian. One thing is utterly certain: Jesus himself instituted it at the Last Supper on the night before his suffering and death, and he gave the commandment that this should be done in memory of him. But although the Eucharist is so new and unique, something specific to Jesus Christ, it nevertheless has deep roots in a preceding history, that is, in the old covenant—and beyond that, in humanity as a whole.

Through the signs that it employs—bread and wine, the gifts of the earth, the fruit of the vine, gifts of the creation—it is woven into the cosmos. It is firmly linked to Jewish history, the history of the old covenant, as we shall see in this chapter. What are the vessels in which the precious treasure was prepared and in which it is still carried and distributed?

One of the genuinely exciting episodes in the history of the Christian churches and of theology has been the rediscovery in the last fifty or hundred years of the Jewish roots of our liturgy. I myself always find it fascinating when scholars help me to discover how much we are supported by the root from which we come (cf. Rom 11:17–18). This not only increases my knowledge, but it also nourishes my faith. This joy is, of course, mingled with regret that this went unrecognized for such a long time and was even explicitly denied. We owe this profound common ground between Jews and Christians to Jesus Christ himself. The Messiah of Israel, the Son of God, is the one who both unites us and separates us. If we love him and follow him on the path he himself took, we cannot detach him from the people from which, as Paul says, he was born "according to the flesh" (Rom 1:3).

The Last Supper and the Old Testament

In his book *Das Abendmahl Jesu als Brennpunkt des Alten Testaments* (The Last Supper of Jesus as the focal point of the Old Testament), the Dominican Adrian Schenker, who is a professor of Old Testament studies, shows the deep relationship between the Eucharist and the Old Testament. We could even say that the Last Supper of Jesus is the "burning glass" in which the Old Testament is concentrated.

In the night before he suffered, Jesus instituted the Eucharist. The first three Gospels tell us that this happened at a *Passover meal*.

In this evening meal, Israel, the chosen people, recalled their liberation from the many years of slavery in Egypt. In this meal, the last meal they took on the evening before they fled out of Egypt is a living reality. This "night of all nights" can be compared only to the Christian Easter Vigil, which has important points of contact with the Jewish Passover. The so-called *seder*, the solemn meal, includes many individual rituals.

Jesus took bread and wine at the points specified in the *seder* ritual. At the beginning, he took the bread, and after the meal in which all had eaten their fill, he took the cup with wine. The evangelist Mark tells us that he spoke a blessing over the bread (14:22). Then came the new words, "Take; this is my body!" At the end of the meal, he took the cup and likewise spoke a prayer over it; Mark calls this a prayer of thanksgiving (14:23). Then he said, "This is my blood of the covenant, which is poured out for many" (14:24).

Let me note at this point that the Church through the centuries has always understood these words just as they were spoken: this *is* my Body; this *is* my Blood. Generations of believers have received Communion in the firm conviction that this *is* the Lord's Body; this *is* his Blood.

Two roots are particularly important for the Eucharist. First, what is the prayer that Jesus spoke at the Last Supper, the prayer that Mark calls blessing and thanksgiving? In the next chapter, we will look at the Passover meal itself.

The Jewish Prayer of Praise and Thanksgiving

> And as they were eating, he took bread, and blessed [*eulogē-sas*], and broke it, and gave it to them, and said, "Take; this is my body." And he took a chalice, and when he had given thanks [*eucharistēsas*] he gave it to them, and they all drank of it. And he said to them, "This is my blood of the covenant, which is poured out for many." (Mk 14:22–24)

One of the two roots of the Eucharist is the *Jewish prayer of praise and thanksgiving*. What does it mean when Mark writes that Jesus spoke the "blessing" over the bread? The Greek verb used here is *eulogēsas*. He spoke the *eulogia* over the bread. He "gave thanks" over the cup—*eucharistēsas*—he spoke the *Eucharist* (Mk 14:22–23). *Eulogia* is translated as "blessing" or "prayer of praise", *eucharistia* as "prayer of thanks". Jesus certainly spoke the Jewish mealtime grace, which is still prayed today and has probably remained basically unaltered since his time. The simple prayer of blessing was usual then; at the Passover meal on the night of liberation, the solemn prayer was used. It is this prayer that has given the Mass one of its names: the "Eucharist".

The Jewish prayers of thanksgiving and praise have a spirituality of their own, and the Eucharist comes from this spiritual root. When one listens attentively to the Jewish tradition, the eucharistic prayers that we hear Sunday after Sunday—the first eucharistic prayer or Roman Canon, the brief second prayer, the longer third prayer, and the very long fourth eucharistic prayer—suddenly sound different. They are prayers of praise and thanksgiving that sound similar to the Jewish act of prayer.

In Yiddish, this kind of prayer is called the *broche*, a word deriving from the Hebrew *berakhah*, which is difficult to translate. A *broche* is a blessing. One who goes to the rabbi and asks for a *broche* is asking for a blessing, just as Catholics will often ask their priest for a blessing. The remarkable thing about this word, however, is that it designates not only a movement from God to us—God blesses us, and we ask for God's blessing—but also a movement from the human person to God. We too can utter a *broche* over God. In other words, we can bless God. This fact may surprise us, but it leads us into the depths of the mystery of the precious treasure that we carry in earthen vessels, namely, the Eucharist.

The prayer that the priest speaks at the offertory, the presentation of the bread and wine, is a *broche* that reproduces almost literally the blessing or praise that is still in use today as the daily Jewish grace at meals. In the liturgy, in a translation that does not entirely capture the original, the priest says:

> Blessed are you, Lord God of all creation,
> for through your goodness we have received
> the bread we offer you:
> fruit of the earth and work of human hands,
> it will become for us the bread of life.

The people respond:

> Blessed be God for ever.

This is the *broche* over the bread. A literal translation of the Hebrew form would run as follows: "*Blessed* are you, Lord our God, Creator of the world, you who bring forth bread from the earth. . . . *Blessed* are you for ever, Lord our God." It may seem a little presumptuous to say that we bless God, but that is in fact what we are doing! In Latin, the word for "blessing" is *benedictio*, and the verb "to bless" is *benedicere*. The *Benedictus* that is prayed every day at Lauds, the Church's

morning prayer, is praise of this kind, a classical *broche*. After
the birth of John the Baptist, the tongue of his father, Zechariah, was loosened and he spontaneously prayed, "*Blessed*
be the Lord God of Israel ..." (Lk 1:68–79). Blessing always
comes from God. Everything that is good comes from his
blessing. But we can thank God and return to him, so to
speak, the blessing that we have received. The Jews understand what we return to him as a blessing: God blesses us,
and we are permitted to bless him in return.

At the beginning of the preface, the priest invites us,
"Let us give thanks to the Lord our God!" In the synagogue, the invitation to prayer is "Gentlemen, let us *bentsch!*"
This Yiddish word comes from *benedicere*, "to bless". We
bless God; we return to him the blessing that we have
received from him. It is the task of the human person, alone
among all creatures, not only to receive God's blessing but
to return it to God as the priest of creation.

The *Benedictus* begins, "Blessed be the Lord God of Israel!"
Zechariah then states the reason for this exhortation: "For
he has visited and redeemed his people" (Lk 1:68). An essential element in the *broche*, the prayer of thanks, is the declaration of the reason for giving thanks. We recall what we
have received, and it is only then that we add a petition. I
say to God, "Look at all we have already received from
you!" And this is followed by a new act of praise. We respond
to the offertory prayer in the words "Blessed be God for
ever." Every Jewish *broche* ends with praise, in the certainty
that God has assured me that I will receive what I have
now asked for, and that he will indeed give it to me. This
means that I can already praise him for it.

There are many such prayers of blessing in the Old Testament. Let me mention only one example. When Moses
killed an Egyptian, he was forced to flee, and he lived in

the wilderness for forty years. After the exodus from Egypt, he came with all the people whom God had rescued from Egypt and led through the Red Sea, and he was reunited with his father-in-law, Jethro. The book of Exodus relates, "Moses told his father-in-law all that the Lord had done to Pharaoh and to the Egyptians for Israel's sake, all the hardship that had come upon them in the way, and how the Lord had delivered them" (18:8). This narrating of the first weeks after the exodus and all that the Israelites had experienced must surely have taken a long time—but people in the Orient have more time than we have! The text then tells us how Moses' father-in-law reacted:

> And Jethro rejoiced for all the good which the LORD had done to Israel, in that he had delivered them out of the hand of the Egyptians.
> And Jethro said, "*Blessed* be the LORD, who has delivered you out of the hand of the Egyptians and out of the hand of Pharaoh. Now I know that the LORD is greater than all gods, because he delivered the people from under the hand of the Egyptians, when they dealt arrogantly with them." And Jethro, Moses' father-in-law, offered a burnt offering and sacrifices to God; and Aaron came with all the elders of Israel to eat bread with Moses' father-in-law before God. (18:9–12; italics added)

This scene anticipates the entire sequence of the eucharistic celebration. We might say that the scene begins with a lengthy "Liturgy of the Word": Moses tells his father-in-law all that God has done by delivering the people in such a marvelous way. First, God brought them out of Egypt in the midst of so many difficulties; then he led them through the Red Sea. Finally, Moses tells him of the time in the wilderness. Jethro's response is a prayer of praise: he intones the "Gloria", the prayer of thanksgiving in which he returns

to God in the act of blessing all the good that God has
done for his son-in-law, Moses, and for the entire people.
They offer sacrifices that express this gratitude and joy. Such
sacrifices are not meant to appease God but to thank him.
This is followed by a joyful meal. Liturgy of the Word,
sacrificial worship, and thanksgiving meal—here, the whole
sequence of the Eucharist is anticipated.

We notice in particular that the sequence begins with
hearing about the mighty deeds of God. The atmosphere
of the *berakhah*, of the *broche*, is thanksgiving and praise
because God does such great things.

There are some very beautiful examples of this in the book
of Tobit. Whenever a great difficulty has to be overcome and
Tobit and Sarah experience God's help, we find a *broche*:
"Blessed is God who lives for ever" and who has rescued us
from this or that situation, the God who has shown us his
faithfulness, the God who did not forget us in our distress.
Indeed, blessed be the Lord, the Almighty (Tob 13:2; cf. 8:15–
17; 11:14, 17; 13:18). This spirituality of the *broche* is an essential element of the soil out of which the Eucharist grew.

The long fourth eucharistic prayer gives us the same experience as Moses and Jethro. The whole story is told (*anamnesis*), beginning with God's act of creation. Human beings
lost their friendship with God, but God did not abandon
them. Again and again, he offered them his covenant and
sent prophets to teach them to look for salvation. Finally,
he sent his Son in order to save them all. This is followed
by the response of praise. Then the sacrifice is made present,
as we shall see below.

First comes *remembering*. The remembrance of God's deeds
is a primal biblical and Jewish action. Remembering makes
us aware that what God did in the past, he will do in the
future also. Since he is faithful, we are entitled to have this

confidence. The past, the present, the future—we experience all this in the Eucharist. We recall what God has done, and we look ahead to what he will do when he comes again in glory. And this now becomes a present reality. Now the Lord is most certainly here. The Eucharist belongs in this sphere of prayer, in an atmosphere of profound trust. We are not afraid of God; rather, we trust in his fidelity.

What makes it possible for people to bless God? The Old Testament replies by affirming that this God is unutterably close to us (cf. Deut 4:7)—but the Old Testament could not yet guess how close he actually is. It was Jesus who first showed us that he is much closer, closer than one can imagine. Indeed, he is so close that he gives us himself as food.

Praise in Daily Life

In Jewish life, the *broche* is important not only in worship in the synagogue or on the great feast days. It also forms a part of daily living. We might call this "eucharistic piety in daily life". One Jewish tradition says that a pious Jew should *bentsch* God one hundred times a day, pronouncing a *broche* over God. Let me mention only a few examples from the tradition of Jewish piety. When one awakes, one should say, "Blessed are you, Lord our God, king of the world. You give the souls back to their mortal bodies, and thus link the morning awakening to the hope of resurrection." The act of getting up in the morning reminds us of the resurrection. When the Jew looks at his surroundings for the first time, he should say, "Blessed are you, Lord our God, king of the world. You open the eyes of the blind." When one gets out of his bed, one should say, "Blessed are you, Lord our God, king of the world. You have established the earth on the waters." And so it continues until one goes to bed in the evening.

This pious tradition helps us to see in a new light the words of the apostle Paul: "Everything created by God is good, and nothing is to be rejected if it is received with *thanksgiving* [*eucharistia* in Greek]; for then it is consecrated by the word of God and prayer" (1 Tim 4:4–5; italics added). Everything is to be Eucharist. Everything is to be given back to God in the prayer of praise, the *broche*.

In the many volumes of the Talmud, which transmit Jewish traditions, we read about the *Berakhot*: "It is forbidden for the human person to enjoy anything that comes from this world without a benediction" (*b. Berakhot* 35a). We should not take anything to ourselves without first speaking an *eucharistia* to God, praising him or—to put it literally—blessing him.

There are many similar *broche* prayers in the life of Jesus too. One impressive example is found in the Gospel of Matthew: "I thank you, Father, Lord of heaven and earth, [*reason:*] that you have hidden these things from the wise and understanding and revealed them to infants; [*summary and praise:*] yes, Father, for such was your gracious will" (11:25–26). Jesus' own piety has its home in the synagogue. Personal piety and the liturgy are closely connected. In our lives too, there should be a real integration of eucharistic prayer and personal prayer.

A Chosen People, a Royal Priesthood

The First Letter of Peter quotes from the book of Exodus: "You are a chosen race, a royal priesthood" (2:9; cf.

Ex 19:5–6). The people of God has a great priestly vocation, both in the Old Testament and in the New. The priest imparts God's blessing and gives the blessing back to God. This task belongs to all the baptized, that is, to the whole people of God. We are to give back to God in the prayer of praise, in the Eucharist, everything that he bestows on us. This is the task not only of the ordained priests; this priestly ministry is the *task of the entire people of God*. God has blessed us, and he expects that the world will be given back to him in the "sacrifice of praise" (Heb 13:15; cf. Ps 50:23).

We read of a discussion in the days of the early Church between a rabbi named Trypho and the Christian Justin, who later suffered martyrdom circa 165. They are debating the following verse from the prophet Malachi: "From the rising of the sun to its setting my name is great among the nations, and in every place incense is offered to my name, and a pure offering; for my name is great among the nations, says the LORD of hosts" (1:11). This passage is echoed in the third eucharistic prayer ("You never cease to gather a people to yourself, so that from the rising of the sun to its setting a pure sacrifice may be offered to your name"), and we believe that wherever on our earth the Eucharist is celebrated, this pure sacrifice is offered to God. The rabbi tells the Christian: Our prayers of *broche*, the numerous prayers of blessing that we utter everywhere on earth, are this "pure sacrifice". It is in this way that we bring the creation back to God in our praise. The Christian replies: No, we believe that the Eucharist of Jesus is the pure sacrifice that is offered to God everywhere on earth from the rising of the sun to its setting. Jesus is himself the perfect *broche* for us, and he offers this *broche* on our behalf. Jesus is God's blessing of the world: "For God so loved the world that he gave his only-begotten Son" for us (Jn 3:16). It is Jesus who has spoken the most perfect *broche* to God, not only through words but through his whole life. He is the perfect priest who has brought everything back to God. And this is the meaning of the Eucharist, which is the perfect sacrifice of praise.

2

HOW DID JESUS CELEBRATE
THE LAST SUPPER?

Our look at the Jewish roots of our liturgy and at their continuing presence in our worship even today shows how marvelously God himself prepared the mystery of the Eucharist in the course of a long history.

Let us now look at how Jesus celebrated the Last Supper. Although the Eucharist is deeply rooted in the Jewish soil, what Jesus did on the evening before his passion was something new—not something imported from another world, so to speak, but something that grows out of what already exists. When we look at it in this light, we can understand it more deeply. The words that Jesus spoke over the bread and the cup of wine are certainly new: "This is my body" and "This is my blood." But he did this in the framework of a Jewish meal, which was probably a Passover meal.

The Last Supper

We have four accounts of what Jesus did on that evening: Matthew 26:26–29, Mark 14:22–25, Luke 22:15–20, and 1 Corinthians 11:23–26. My starting point here will be the account by the evangelist Luke. It is not so important whether this—or perhaps the account by the evangelist Mark—is the most original narrative, since all four accounts agree on the essential points, stating briefly what Jesus did on the eve of his passion.

Jesus sent some disciples to prepare the upper room for the meal, in accordance with the tradition. At that period, people ate the Passover lying on cushions in an upper room on the second floor of a house. They stood for the central part of the meal. After the disciples had prepared the meal, Jesus went up with them to the second floor and celebrated the Passover with them. The evangelist Luke writes:

> And he said to them, "I have earnestly desired to eat this Passover with you before I suffer; for I tell you I shall not eat it until it is fulfilled in the kingdom of God." And he took a chalice, and when he had given thanks he said, "Take this, and divide it among yourselves; for I tell you that from now on I shall not drink of the fruit of the vine until the kingdom of God comes." And he took bread, and when he had given thanks he broke it and gave it to them, saying, "This is my body which is given for you. Do this in remembrance of me." And likewise the chalice after supper, saying, "This chalice which is poured out for you is the new covenant in my blood." (22:15–20)

The other accounts make some additions. For example, we read in Matthew that the Blood "is poured out for many for the forgiveness of sins" (26:28).

Let us look more closely at Luke's text. The first, and most important, sentence here is "I have earnestly desired [literally, "With desire I have desired"] to eat this Passover with you before I suffer." For every believing Jew, it is a great joy to celebrate the Passover, and something for which he longs. This is the feast of feasts, the night of liberation, the night on which the people recall how they went forth from Egypt and were freed from the house of slavery. It is a feast full of expectancy and joy. For Jesus, this Passover looks to the future: it is full of expectancy, for he knows that he will soon suffer. It is a farewell meal that looks ahead to what will come: "I shall not eat it until it is fulfilled in the kingdom of God." He now takes the first cup (which only Luke mentions), gives thanks, and says, "Take this, and divide it among yourselves; for I tell you that from now on I shall not drink of the fruit of the vine until the kingdom of God comes." He looks ahead with longing to the coming of the kingdom of God.

It is only now that we read those words that are so familiar to us. Jesus takes bread, gives thanks, breaks the bread, and gives it to the apostles with the words that the Church has heard again and again from then on: "This is my body which is given for you. Do this in remembrance of me." Between the bread that Jesus breaks and the cup that he gives his disciples lies the Last Supper in the strict sense of the term, the Passover meal. At the end of this meal, he once again takes a cup with wine—this is the cup with which we are familiar—and speaks the following words: "This chalice which is poured out for you is the new covenant in my blood."

A Passover Meal

Scholars debate whether or not this farewell meal of Jesus was the Passover meal. The chronology is rather difficult, with divergent data in John and the three other evangelists, and various interpretations have been proposed. It is certain that this meal of Jesus took place in the context of the Passover feast in Jerusalem, at a time when the city was full of pilgrims. It has been estimated that an immense crowd, as many as one hundred thousand pilgrims from all of Israel and the Diaspora, may have been there. The high point was the Passover meal and then the Passover feast in the temple.

In the evening Mass on Holy Thursday, we hear the account of the institution of the Passover feast from the book of Exodus (12:1–8, 11–14). Every family is to take a one-year-old male lamb without blemish and slaughter it in the evening. The doorposts are to be smeared with the blood of this lamb. On the same night, they are to eat its flesh, roasted over the fire. It is to be eaten "with unleavened bread and bitter herbs"; it is to be eaten "in haste", and nothing is to be left over (cf. 12:5–11). "In this manner you shall eat it: your loins girded, your sandals on your feet, and your staff in your hand; and you shall eat it in haste. It is the LORD's Passover. For I will pass through the land of Egypt that night, and I will strike all the first-born in the land of Egypt" (12:11–12). On this night, Israel was freed from Egypt. They departed in such great haste that they did not even have the time to bake their bread.

> So the people took their dough before it was leavened, their kneading bowls being bound up in their mantles on their shoulders.... And they baked unleavened cakes of the dough which they had brought out of Egypt, for it was not leavened, because they were thrust out of Egypt and could not tarry, neither had they prepared for themselves any provisions. (12:34, 39)

All this plays an important role in determining how the Passover has been celebrated down to the present day by our Jewish fellow citizens. "It was a night of watching by the LORD, to bring them out of the land of Egypt" (12:42).

God tells Moses and Aaron, "This is the ordinance of the Passover" (12:43). When they enter the promised land and celebrate the feast of unleavened bread and recall their departure from the house of slavery in Egypt, they must then tell their children about this. "And you shall tell your son on that day, 'It is because of what the LORD did for me when I came out of Egypt'" (13:8).

The Jewish tradition has continued to celebrate the *seder* in this way. There are many editions of the texts of the *Passover Haggadah*, that is, the rubrics of the Passover rite, which includes the questions that the children must ask: "What does all this mean? Why do we do this?" The answers prescribed in the rubrics tell them: We do this to recall how our ancestors went forth from Egypt.

When we read the ritual of the *seder*, the liturgy of the Passover meal, we can understand why the evangelist Luke speaks of a first cup. The evening begins with blessings pronounced over the first cup of wine, the so-called *kiddush* cup. Jesus links his words of longing to this first cup: "I have earnestly desired to eat this Passover with you!"

The ritual continues with what is described in the book of Exodus: bitter herbs and unleavened bread (*matzo*) are eaten. One rite, which may not go as far back as the time of Jesus, is particularly impressive. Three *matzo* loaves lie on the table. The father of the house takes one piece away from the middle loaf and hides it. The Jewish tradition sees this bread (*afikoman*), which is first hidden and then brought forth, as a symbol of the longed-for Messiah: as yet, he is hidden, but he will come. The entire evening is full of longing and expectancy. The participants look back to what happened in the past, but they also look to the future, and above all to the Messiah who is to come. When the father of the house breaks the *matzo* loaves, he utters the blessing of bread. And it is precisely at this point, at this blessing of bread before the meal, that Jesus spoke the words we know so well. Just as the bread is shared among those present at every Jewish meal, and especially at the Passover, so Jesus too shared bread among his disciples. We shall see below what this means.

> And when in time to come your son asks you, "What does this mean?" you shall say to him, "By strength of hand the LORD brought us out of Egypt, from the house of bondage." (Ex 13:14)

A second cup of wine is now drunk, and then comes the narrative. The youngest child asks questions: "What does this mean? What is the meaning of the unleavened bread and the bitter herbs?" The father relates the story of the exodus and explains why they are eating bitter herbs and unleavened bread on this evening. After the *matzo* bread has been distributed, the meal properly speaking begins. After the meal, the third cup is poured. It was over this third cup that Jesus spoke the words that we hear at every Mass: "This is the chalice of my Blood, the Blood of the new and eternal covenant."

All this is profoundly symbolic. Let me quote only a few words from the explanation that children and adults are given in the *Passover Haggadah*:

> The Passover sacrifice that our ancestors ate, as long as the holy temple stood—what was the reason for it? Because the Holy One, praised be he, had passed over the houses of our ancestors in Egypt, as it is written: "You shall say, 'It is the sacrifice of the LORD's Passover, for he passed over the houses of the sons of Israel in Egypt, when he slew the Egyptians but spared our houses.'" (Ex 12:27)

The *Passover Haggadah* calls the meal a Passover *sacrifice*. Many people can no longer understand this. Why do we call the Mass a sacrifice, not only a meal? We shall return to this below.

When the children ask what the *matzo* loaves of unleavened bread mean, the father replies:

> It is because our ancestors did not have time to leaven their dough, since the King of all kings, the Holy One, praised be he, had already revealed himself to them and redeemed them. For so it is written: "And they baked unleavened cakes of the dough which they had brought out of Egypt, for it was not leavened, because they were thrust out of Egypt and could not tarry, neither had they prepared for themselves any provisions." (Ex 12:39)

The child then asks, "And why do we eat bitter herbs, the *maror*?"

> It is because the Egyptians made our ancestors' life bitter, as it is written: "They made their lives bitter with hard service, in mortar and brick, and in all kinds of work in the field; in all their work they made them serve with rigor." (Ex 1:14)

This is the native soil in which our Eucharist grew.

The Breaking of the Bread

To begin with, we have the rite of the *breaking of the bread*, which clearly so impressed the early Christians that they used this as a name for the Eucharist. We read about the earliest community in Jerusalem, "They held steadfastly to the apostles' teaching and fellowship, to the breaking of the bread and to the prayers" (Acts 2:42), and a little later, "They broke bread in their homes" (2:46).

> They [the disciples] constrained him, saying, "Stay with us, for it is toward evening and the day is now far spent." So he went in to stay with them. When he was at table with them, he took the bread and blessed and broke it, and gave it to them. And their eyes were opened and they recognized him; and he vanished out of their sight. (Lk 24:29–31)

We all know the Emmaus story (Lk 24:13–35). Two disciples walked beside Jesus, who accompanied them and explained the scriptures to them, showing why things had to happen as they did. They did not recognize him. They began to eat, and he took the bread—and Luke tells us specifically that they recognized him by means of the gesture of breaking the bread.

The breaking of bread was a perfectly normal gesture at the beginning of every meal. This was the official opening of the meal, so to speak. All who were at table received a share of the broken bread. I myself have experienced this among Arabs in the Middle East. The broken bread is the sign of table fellowship. Through the breaking of the bread, those who receive and eat a piece of the bread are united to form a community. However, this gesture has an even deeper meaning in the Jewish tradition: it also imparts a blessing. A blessing, with a familiar ring, is spoken over the bread: "Blessed are you, Lord our God, king of the world. You bring forth bread from the earth." The prayer of praise uttered over the bread at the offertory in the Eucharist has a very similar wording.

Those who receive a piece of bread belong to the community of blessing. The Hebrew word for this fellowship is *chaburah*. In an age of fast food, we have forgotten what table fellowship truly means. In the Old Testament, one of the worst breaches of trust occurs when one table companion raises his hand against another, or betrays him. Judas' betrayal is made even worse by the fact that it happens after Jesus has given him the piece of bread that bestows a share in fellowship; it is at that very moment that Judas goes out and betrays the Master (Jn 13:30).

We can also grasp why people took offense at Jesus' table fellowship with tax collectors and sinners. When he sits down at table with sinners, he is offering them the peace that comes from fellowship with God. That is exactly what Jesus intends—and that is exactly what gives offense.

The Bible also shows us the gravity of exclusion from table fellowship: this is a metaphor for eternal damnation. One who cannot take his place at the meal in the kingdom of God is excluded forever. This is why Jesus says in one of his parables that when the bridegroom comes, the door will be shut from the inside. The wedding feast is celebrated, and the table fellowship is formed. Some people then come and want to enter. They knock and say, "Lord, we ate and drank in your presence!" But he will answer, "I do not know where you come from" (Lk 13:25–27; cf. Mt 25:10–12). We also read, "Blessed is he who shall eat bread in the kingdom of God!" (Lk 14:15). This metaphor depicts the perfection of fellowship: to eat bread in the kingdom of God.

There is a mysterious passage in the book of Exodus that relates that after the covenant between God and the people was made at Mount Sinai, the people and the altar (as the symbol of God) were sprinkled with blood; we shall see in the next chapter what this means. The text continues:

> Then Moses and Aaron, Nadab, and Abihu, and seventy of the elders of Israel went up, and they saw the God of Israel;

and there was under his feet as it were a pavement of sap-
phire stone, like the very heaven for clearness. And he did
not lay his hand on the chief men of the people of Israel;
they beheld God, and ate and drank. (Ex 24:9–11)

This is the most concentrated expression in the Old Testament of the mystery of the Eucharist, and this helps us to
understand why the Acts of the Apostles says, referring to
the Jewish and early Christian meals, but above all to the
Lord's Supper, "They partook of food with glad . . . hearts"
(2:46)—for those who are permitted to eat and drink in
the presence of God have every reason to be glad.

Prayers of Thanksgiving

After the breaking of bread comes the Passover meal. The
lamb is accompanied on this day with all kinds of herbs,
eggs, and vegetables. The ritual concludes with three solemn prayers of blessing in which God is thanked for the
food that has been eaten, especially for the bread; for the
land and the earth; and for Jerusalem, the city of God. All
these elements will be found later on in Christian prayer,
in the Eucharist. The thanksgiving begins, "Let us praise
the Lord, from whose good things we have been nourished" (*m. Berakhot* 7:3; in the previous chapter, I recalled
the preface at Mass, which begins the eucharistic prayer
with the words "Let us give thanks to the Lord our God!").
Then come the three prayers of blessing.

The first *broche* is a prayer of praise and thanksgiving for
the food that has been received. God is thanked above all
for his providence and for his mercy; he never forgets any of
his creatures. Let me quote briefly from this prayer: "Blessed
are you, Lord our God, king of the world. In his goodness he

nourishes the whole world with grace, fidelity, and mercy. He gives food to all flesh, for his grace lasts forever."

The second prayer gives thanks for the land and for the earth. This refers, of course, primarily to the promised land, but it also thanks God for all that he did when he brought his people into this land: "We thank you, Lord our God, because you let our ancestors inherit a lovely, good, and broad land, and because you led us out of the land of Egypt and redeemed us from the house of slavery.... And for everything we thank you, Lord our God, and praise you." Thanksgiving for salvation history, for redemption—this is precisely what we do in the eucharistic prayer. We thank God for everything that he did to redeem us and set us free.

Finally, the third prayer thanks God for Jerusalem. This includes a prayer for the future: "Have mercy, Lord our God, upon Israel your people, and upon Jerusalem your city, and upon Zion where your glory dwells, and upon the kingdom of the house of David your anointed one, and upon the great and holy house over which your name is named." This is the yearning that God may indeed bring about his kingdom: "Thy kingdom come!" In the Passover meal, it is expressed in the acclamation "This year in foreign parts, next year in Jerusalem!" In our Christian prayer, this has become the acclamation of longing "We proclaim your Death, O Lord, ... *until you come again*" (italics added).

Bella Chagall (the wife of the painter Marc Chagall), in her memoirs of her childhood, speaks very beautifully of this longing for the coming of the Messiah. She relates how at one point in the Passover meal, the youngest child must go to the door and open it, looking out into the dark night— perhaps the Messiah is standing before the door! We encounter the same deep longing in the Gospel, when people in Jerusalem ask one another, "What do you think? That Jesus

will not come to the feast?" (Jn 11:56), and then go out to
meet him when they hear that he is coming to Jerusalem
(12:12). The hope is that the Messiah will come during this
night, the night of the Passover, for it was on a Passover
night that Israel was liberated from Egypt. This yearning
for God to inaugurate his reign has never disappeared from
the Church. "Maranatha! Come, Lord Jesus!" (1 Cor 16:22;
Rev 22:20; *Didache* 10.6); this acclamation of the early Christians has its roots in Jewish tradition, which longed for the
coming of the Messiah.

A Meal, and More Than a Meal

When we read these texts, we see where our prayers in the
Mass come from. It is wonderful to see how God himself
has prepared the celebration in which we are permitted to
take part. Above all, we can understand better the new element that Jesus introduced that evening. I am profoundly
saddened when I note how little understanding we Christians have for the life of the Jewish people, for although
not all of them have accepted Jesus as Messiah and Savior,
they remain the chosen people.

These reflections on the Passover make it very clear that
the Eucharist is not simply a meal. The bread that is broken and the cup that is blessed come at the beginning and
the end of the meal; they are not themselves a meal that is
meant to satisfy one's hunger. The apostle Paul does not
mince words in his criticism of the Corinthians:

> When you meet together, it is not the Lord's supper that
> you eat. For in eating, each one goes ahead with his own
> meal, and one is hungry and another is drunk. What! Do

you not have houses to eat and drink in? Or do you despise the Church of God and humiliate those who have nothing? What shall I say to you? Shall I commend you in this? No, I will not. (1 Cor 11:20–22)

The apostle then warns:

Any one who eats and drinks without discerning the body eats and drinks judgment upon himself. (1 Cor 11:29)

The Eucharist is not just a meal to provide nourishment. It is celebrated on an altar; and although that altar is indeed a table, it is more than a table. The Eucharist is something unique. It is a *sacrificial meal*. We know very little about how the earliest Church celebrated it, but one thing is certain: it bore the marks of Jewish prayer and celebration. If we wish to understand what then gradually developed into the liturgy we celebrate today, we need to know something about this background.

Synopsis of the Words over the Bread

Mt 26:26

As they were eating, Jesus took bread, and blessed, and broke it, and gave it to the disciples and said, "Take, eat; this is my body."

Mk 14:22

As they were eating, he took bread, and blessed, and broke it, and gave it to them, and said, "Take; this is my body."

Lk 22:19

And he took bread, and when he had given thanks he broke it and gave it them, saying, "This is my body

1 Cor 11:23–24

The Lord Jesus on the night when he was betrayed took bread, and when he had given thanks, he broke it, which is given for you. Do this in remembrance of me."

and said, "This is my body which is for you. Do this in remembrance of me."

Synopsis of the Words over the Cup

Mt 26:27–28

And he took a chalice, and when he had given thanks he gave it to them, saying, "Drink of it, all of you; for this is my blood of the covenant, which is poured out for many for the forgiveness of sins."

Mk 14:23–24

And he took a chalice, and when he had given thanks he gave it to them, and they all drank of it. And he said to them, "This is my blood of the covenant, which is poured out for many."

Lk 22:20

And likewise the chalice after supper, saying, "This chalice which is poured out for you is the new covenant in my blood."

1 Cor 11:25

In the same way also the chalice, after supper, saying, "This chalice is the new covenant in my blood. Do this, as often as you drink it, in remembrance of me."

3

"THIS IS MY BODY; THIS IS MY BLOOD"

"This is my body." "This is my blood." Around these two new sayings, there is born the rite that Christians have celebrated from the very beginning under the names of "the breaking of the bread" and "the Lord's Supper", and soon also "the Eucharist". In the present chapter, we shall look at these "words of institution" (which we also call the "words of consecration").

> Lord Jesus Christ, you have given us the most precious thing you could give: your own self in your Eucharist. Let us recognize more deeply what the faith tells us. Let us live more deeply what you yourself give us. Amen.

General Issues

Our question is: What did Jesus mean by these words? Is it at all possible, two thousand years later, to know what he meant? Indeed, are we really certain that he said these words in this way? The great dispute from the very beginning has been about whether Jesus meant these words literally or symbolically. Did he say that "this"—the bread that he broke—was his body in some symbolic sense, or was it *really* his body that he gave to the disciples?

How can we settle this question? We can approach it from three angles, and when we see how these complement one another, we can be certain about what Jesus meant.

First, let us ask about the meaning of Jesus' words and actions. What do we learn here from philology (the academic study of languages) and exegesis (the academic study of scripture)?

There is, of course, one great difficulty: there is no audio recording of Jesus' words. What we have are *four different accounts*, in Matthew 26:26–29, Mark 14:22–25, Luke 22:15–20, and 1 Corinthians 11:23–26, and each of these gives a slightly different version of these words. This could be taken as a sign that we have no exact knowledge, but it is also possible to argue that the core of the narrative can be trusted, since all four texts say exactly the same thing, with only slight variations in the wording. When the testimony of four separate witnesses is in substantial agreement, their story is credible. And this means that we can really hear the words of Jesus in these four accounts. They are a mirror, so to speak, that shows what Jesus intended.

Second, we have access via the *tradition* that has been handed on in the Church. From the very beginning, the Church has obeyed Jesus' command: "They broke bread in their homes" (Acts 2:46). The four texts in Matthew, Mark, Luke, and 1 Corinthians were written later. Scholars disagree about the exact date of composition of these texts. Paul probably wrote to the Corinthians in the 50s of the first century; some exegetes believe that the three Gospels were written before the year 70, while others prefer a later date. In any case, a lengthy period has intervened between the Last Supper and the writing of these texts, and they give us a glimpse of how the Christian communities celebrated the Lord's Supper, the Eucharist.

Paul writes to the community in Corinth, where a conflict has arisen. When they meet for the Lord's Supper, some eat a great deal while others have nothing to eat. Indeed, says Paul, some members of the community are drunk, while others are still hungry. Disorder reigns in Corinth, and Paul must therefore remind them what he had taught them. He affirms in simple and clear words, "For I received from the Lord what I also delivered to you." We do not know how he received this from the Lord, since Paul was not present at the Last Supper. But he heard very early on what Jesus had done on that evening, and now he hands it on again to others.

> The Lord Jesus on the night when he was betrayed took bread, and when he had given thanks, he broke it, and said, "This is my body which is for you. Do this in remembrance of me." In the same way also the chalice, after supper, saying, "This chalice is the new covenant in my blood. Do this, as often as you drink it, in remembrance of me." (1 Cor 11:23–25)

These words were used in Corinth at the celebration of the Lord's Supper. The three other accounts reflect likewise the wording that was in use in the early Church. Mark probably heard them from Peter, and Matthew presents the customary wording in the communities in Palestine; Luke has almost the same wording as the apostle Paul. What we read in the New Testament is thus already *tradition*. In the Gospels, we find what the Church lived at that period, in the first twenty, thirty, or forty years.

It is obvious that nothing was handed on so carefully and exactly as the words of Jesus, especially the words of consecration that he spoke at the Last Supper. And no moment in the Mass is more solemn than the moment when the priest repeats the words of Jesus.

It is the bishop's task to ensure that the liturgy is celebrated correctly in the parishes. Sometimes bishops are rather too tolerant in this field, but on one point there is an absolutely rigorous consensus: no experiments are allowed on the words of consecration. The words are sacred! And the primary reason for this sacredness is because their meaning is so important.

We celebrate what Jesus celebrated at the Last Supper in the upper room. This tradition is very reliable; it has not been "doctored" in the course of the centuries. It is true that the celebration of the Mass has undergone a tremendous development, and I do not know whether the Corinthian community would feel at home today in the Mass we celebrate in Saint Stephen's Cathedral—or whether we would feel at home in the community in Corinth. But one thing is certain: the words spoken by the presider of the Eucharist over the bread and the wine, both then and now, are the same words. Paul and the evangelists hand them on with great fidelity.

The astounding thing is that the great tradition of the Church, now two thousand years old, in its reflections on the meaning of these words—"This is my body; this is my blood"—has understood them not as a mere symbol but as the literal truth: this *is* my Body; this *is* my Blood. It is more than a sign that helps us to recall Jesus.

This is what we mean when we say in the Mass, "The mystery of faith." Sometimes the priest says, "This is *a* mystery of the faith", but that is incorrect. It is *the* mystery of our faith that is celebrated in the liturgy.

We are kneeling, and the priest genuflects. He is assuredly not genuflecting in front of a mere symbol! We shall return to this below in chapter 6, when we speak of the consecration.

There is a *third* path that makes us certain of what Jesus intended, namely, *experience*. Up to the present day, people have experienced again and again that the words of Jesus are really true. Sometimes these experiences have been exceptional: people have lived for years on end with the Eucharist as their only nourishment. Famous examples are Saint Catherine of Siena (died 1380), whose only food for years was Holy Communion, and Saint Nicholas of Flüe (died 1487), the patron saint of Switzerland. An impressive example from our own days is the stigmatic Marthe Robin (died 1981), who likewise lived for many years on the Eucharist alone. Such exceptional situations are signs that it is the Lord himself who gives himself to us as our nourishment.

In addition to these great mystical experiences, there is also the daily experience that the eucharistic Body of Jesus is truly nourishment for us and that it contains our life: Jesus truly comes to us in the Eucharist and gives us life.

When I was a young theological student, I once said to my aunt, "I have my problems with the Eucharist, with the Mass." At that period, in the 1960s, a whole range of theories were asserting that no genuine consecration took place and that Jesus' words meant something different. As a young student, I drank all this in and proudly told my aunt about it. She gave me a sad look and said, "If you take away the Eucharist from us, you take away everything from us." That was not some theoretical affirmation, a piece of dry dogma that she had picked up somewhere. It was her life! And I will never forget that conversation.

Ultimately, it is the Holy Spirit who tells us what Jesus really meant when he spoke those words. He speaks to us through the scriptures; he is at work in the tradition of the Church; and he is present in our experience. He keeps the understanding of the Eucharist alive in believers.

Symbolic and Real Actions: "This Is My Body"

Jesus said the following words, probably in Aramaic or Hebrew, over the bread: "This is my body", and he probably added, "for you", or even, "given for you". At first sight, this appears clear and simple. Jesus takes the bread, blesses it, breaks it, and gives it to his disciples. He genuinely means that what he is giving them is his body. The bread that is broken and shared is Jesus himself, his body that he lays down in death for us, the body that will be crucified—and he gives us his body in order that we may share in him. I believe that most of those who go to Mass on Sunday understand the words of Jesus in this way, but there are objections and difficulties to which we must now turn, since faith must never shrink from challenges and difficulties.

To begin with, there are linguistic difficulties. In Hebrew, the word "is" does not exist. Jesus did not say "This is my body" but "This my body." However, this is certainly not an insuperable problem.

One common objection is that this action and these words of Jesus were meant to *depict* something. There are many symbolic actions in the Old Testament, and it is clear that Jesus stood in this tradition. Let me mention three examples of symbolic actions by the prophet Ezekiel. God tells him, "Prepare for yourself an exile's baggage" (12:3). Ezekiel does so. On the evening of the same day, God says, "Dig through the wall in their sight, and go out through it" (12:5). He does this before the eyes of the people of Jerusalem, who then ask him, "What are you doing?" God tells Ezekiel, "Say, 'I am a sign for you: as I have done, so shall it be done to them; they shall go into exile, into captivity'" (12:11). By means of his symbolic action, Ezekiel is telling the Israelites that this is going to happen to them.

And so the objection runs, was not Jesus' Last Supper too an action of this kind? Did he not perhaps wish to say, "As this bread is broken now, so my body will be broken in death. As this bread is distributed now, so I give my life for you"? And is not this a beautiful symbol?

Another passage is even clearer. Ezekiel is given the following command:

> And you, O son of man, take a sharp sword; use it as a barber's razor and pass it over your head and your beard; then take balances for weighing, and divide the hair. A third part you shall burn in the fire in the midst of the city, when the days of the siege are completed; and a third part you shall take and strike with the sword round about the city; and a third part you shall scatter to the wind, and I will unsheathe the sword after them. And you shall take from these a small number, and bind them in the skirts of your robe. And of these again you shall take some, and cast them into the fire, and burn them in the fire; from there a fire will come forth into all the house of Israel. (5:1–4)

The symbolic language here seems strange, but Ezekiel is told that he must then tell the people of Israel, "Thus says the Lord God: *This is Jerusalem*" (5:5; italics added). This sounds exactly like the words that Jesus said: "This is my body."

God continues, "I have set her in the center of the nations, with countries round about her. And she has wickedly rebelled against my ordinances more than the nations, and against my statutes more than the countries round about her" (5:5–6). This is why they will be scattered like the hairs that Ezekiel scatters.

Is not this situation similar to what Jesus did? May not the breaking and distributing of the bread be a symbolic action like that of Ezekiel? And does not this interpretation find support in Jesus' command "Do this in remembrance of me", that is, "Repeat this sign, so that you will remember me"?

However, this sign of the prophet Ezekiel is more than a merely symbolic action. When the prophet does something with his own hair, this is more than just a sign that something will later happen to Jerusalem. In a certain sense, he is already anticipating God's judgment, since his hair that is scattered and burned is itself a part (even if only a tiny part) of Jerusalem. To use a Christian theological term, it is a *sacrament* of Jerusalem: what happens on the small scale to the hair will happen to the city as a whole.

What Jesus did certainly signifies his death. He breaks the bread, as happens at every Jewish meal, and then he says, "See, this has a new meaning. This is my body, which will be broken in death." But it is more than a sign. What Jesus gives the disciples is already a part of what is about to happen. He gives them even now a share in his own body. This is how Christians have always understood his words, and this is how we understand them still.

There is an important difference between the actions of Ezekiel and Jesus here. The prophet performed his symbolic action with only a small part of Jerusalem, a few hairs. We believe that Jesus gives himself completely in the bread—not just a part of himself. This is truly his body, Jesus in person.

"My Blood, the Blood of the Covenant"

Here too it is helpful to look at the precise words that Jesus spoke over the cup of wine, but this is more difficult, because they are transmitted in two different versions. In Mark, we read, "This is my blood of the covenant, which is poured out for many" (14:24); Matthew adds, "for the forgiveness of sins" (26:28). The other form is found in Luke: "This chalice which is poured out for you is the new covenant in my blood" (22:20), and more briefly in Paul: "This chalice is the new covenant in my blood" (1 Cor 11:25). It is difficult, indeed almost impossible, to answer the question, what words did Jesus literally use? But the elements are invariable: *blood, covenant, poured out, for you/for many.*

Once again, we need to look at the Jewish roots. Believing Jews would have recognized here echoes of three important concepts from the Old Testament, when Jesus speaks of the *blood of the covenant,* the *new covenant,* and the *covenant in my blood.*

First, when Moses received the law, the Ten Commandments, from God and proclaimed them to the Israelites, the whole people replied, "All the words which the LORD has spoken we will do" (Ex 24:3). Moses then took twelve stones, symbolizing the twelve tribes of Israel, and built an altar on which sacrifices were offered. "And Moses took half of the blood [of the sacrificed beasts] and put it in basins, and half of the blood he threw against the altar" (24:6). Moses read the book of the covenant to the people, who answered, "All that the LORD has spoken we will do, and we will be obedient" (24:7). Moses then took the blood from the basin "and threw it upon the people, and said, 'Behold the blood of the covenant which the LORD

has made with you in accordance with all these words'"
(24:8).

What is the meaning of the blood on the altar, the blood
with which he sprinkles the people? The covenant is made
with blood. Blood is life; when the blood is removed, life
is removed. When the blood is poured out, a human being
dies. This is why the covenant is made with blood. In the
old covenant, the altar symbolizes God, just as our altar
symbolizes Christ for us. Moses sprinkles the altar and the
people with the blood of the sacrificed animals in order to
demonstrate that there is now a covenant, a stable covenant
of life between God and his people, who are joined together
forever.

The "blood of the covenant" is an obvious reminiscence
of this event on Mount Sinai. Jesus makes a covenant with
his disciples by taking blood—his own Blood!—and sharing it with them, giving it to them to drink. We shall see
that it is not easy to understand this in a purely "spiritual"
sense.

Second, this covenant was repeatedly broken. God had
made the covenant, but his people did not keep it. The
prophet Jeremiah promises that a time will come when
there will be a *new covenant*, one that will never again be
broken:

> Behold, the days are coming, says the LORD, when I will
> make a new covenant with the house of Israel and the house
> of Judah, not like the covenant which I made with their
> fathers when I took them by the hand to bring them
> out of the land of Egypt, my covenant which they broke.
> (Jer 31:31–32)

Since they have broken this covenant, God will give a new
covenant:

But this is the covenant which I will make with the house of Israel after those days, says the LORD: I will put my law within them, and I will write it on their hearts; and I will be their God, and they shall be my people. (Jer 31:33)

Jesus says, "This is the new covenant in my blood."

Third, the fact that Jesus says "This is *my* blood" is especially impressive. "My blood" means: "This is I myself." There is only one passage in the Old Testament where a human being is called "covenant"—the great text that we read on Good Friday each year, the fourth song of the Servant of Yahweh in Isaiah (Is 52–53). Somewhat earlier, God says of his Servant:

I am the LORD, I have called you in righteousness,
I have taken you by the hand and kept you;
I have given you as a covenant to the people,
a light to the nations. (42:6)

The Servant of the Lord is the covenant in person.

What words rang in Jesus' ears, so to speak, and what was in his heart when he spoke these mysterious words over the bread and the wine? Most probably, he was thinking of these obscure prophecies about the Servant of Yahweh. The fourth song says that the Servant is "bruised" and "put to grief". The Servant of Yahweh "poured out his soul to death". The next words are very important for the Mass: "He makes himself an offering for sin". We are familiar with this idea: "Lamb of God, you take away the sins of the world ..." "He bore the sin of many, and made intercession for the transgressors" (Is 53:10, 12). We find all this already in the prophet Isaiah.

When we consider all the echoes of the Old Testament in the words that Jesus speaks over the cup, we see that he himself is the covenant that is now being made in the Blood that he sheds for us, for the "many".

Not to Be Taken for Granted

Is this to be understood symbolically, or in a very literal sense? One little remark in Mark's account is striking: the evangelist tells us that Jesus gave them the cup "and they all drank of it" (14:23). Why does he mention this detail? It is because the disciples are Jews—and this is an extraordinarily difficult thing for a believing Jew, who has learned from the very first pages of the Bible that one is not allowed to drink blood. Blood is sacred because blood is life. The commandment not to drink blood is one of the strictest prohibitions in the old covenant. To drink blood is to commit a grave offense. This shows that it cannot have been easy to accept these words of Jesus.

Sometimes I wonder what people who come into our cathedral think—people who may never have taken part in a Mass and then hear these words: "This is the chalice of my Blood, the Blood of the new and eternal covenant." They hear the dialogue: "The Blood of Christ.—Amen" and see people drinking from the chalice. It is easy to see why many feel a sense of revulsion and say, "This cannot be meant literally! One cannot drink blood!"

People in the earliest times reacted in three different ways. The Jewish reaction is expressed clearly in the Gospel of John, when Jesus is still in Galilee. Jesus tells the people in the synagogue at Capernaum that he is "the bread of life" and affirms, "He who eats my flesh and drinks my blood abides in me, and I in him" (Jn 6:48, 56). He says, "My flesh is food indeed, and my blood is drink indeed", and the reaction is unambiguous: "This is a hard saying; who can listen to it?" (6:55, 60). Many who hear this discourse leave him, although they had sympathized with him up to then; John underlines that it is "many of his *disciples*" who say, "This is a hard saying", and that "many of his *disciples* drew back and no longer walked with him" (6:60, 66; italics added). This reaction is so widespread that Jesus finally asks the closest circle of his friends, the Twelve, "Will you also go away?" (6:67).

The Gentiles, who do not come from the Jewish tradition, react with shock or mockery. They laugh at the very idea. It has been suggested that the *Satyricon* of the Roman satirist Petronius (died 66) is a parody of the Lord's Supper. The pagans asserted that the Christians were cannibals who ate the flesh of their god and drank his blood—a weird religion!

It is not easy to understand what Jesus did at the Last Supper in the upper room. Was it intended only symbolically, or did Jesus mean it in an utterly realistic sense? There is a third reaction: the Christian tradition has always understood his actions and his words realistically. The bread and wine truly become his Body and Blood, and faith accepts this. Faith is not always simple, and the Lord has not spared us the hard work of believing. In a sense, he asks us too, "Will you also go away? Or can you accept this as the most marvelous gift of my love? My gift of myself to you is so complete that you can live from it."

4

"DO THIS IN MEMORY OF ME"

What does Jesus mean when he commands the disciples "Do this in memory of me"? Let me begin by looking at the question: What does remembering mean? We shall then ask: When he says these words, what exactly is the Lord commanding us to do? Finally, we shall ask how the early Church celebrated this remembrance of Jesus, and we will see that the structures from the earliest times have survived down to the present day.

Remembrance

Many monuments recall the victims of the two great twentieth-century wars. We recall the anniversary of the foundation of an institution, of a wedding, or of a priestly ordination; and we recall birthdays. These are memorial celebrations. Is it this kind of remembrance Jesus intends when he says "Do this in memory of me"? It is, of course, true that the Eucharist is a memorial celebration, and the texts of the Mass make us aware of this fact: "On the night he was betrayed he himself took bread . . ." This is the remembrance of one specific event, namely, Jesus' Last Supper and the passion and Resurrection that followed.

What does it mean to remember? In our monastery, there lived a man who had lost his memory through meningitis. He worked in the house, swept the corridors, and cleaned the rooms. He always had a list of the things to be done, and he put a tick against every task he had finished, because even only a few minutes later, he no longer knew whether or not he had done it. When illness deprives a person of his memory, he loses something essential. He is handed over to the tyranny of the present moment, so to speak, because both past and future are meaningless. He can find no continuities in his life. A decisive element in human life is our ability to make the past become present anew in our memory. I can recall scenes from my life—good or bad, guilty or virtuous—and they become present in my memory as if I were experiencing them now. It can also happen that something suddenly pops up out of my memory. For years on end, I have not thought about it, and then suddenly it is there. I recall a past situation, a moment in my life, and it becomes present. I would be like a cork bobbing aimlessly on the surface if the individual moments in my life were not linked together by memory to form a biography. This is why memory is so important; and I myself note that with the passing of the years, memory becomes even more important. When I was a young man, that seemed a strange idea; but for one thing, there is now more to remember, and for another, I am astonished to see how the earlier events in my own life become more present and more vivid. Without this continuity in my life—this ability to link the past and the present together—there is no real future.

Remembering always involves the act of remembering in common. Forty years after my high school graduation, my class came together, and I met some of my former classmates for the first time in forty years. I looked at one of them—his hair was almost white. He asked, "Don't you remember me? I sat behind you in class." And suddenly I saw in the man's face the features of the boy he was forty years ago. We were united by the experiences we had shared, and collective memories of this kind create community. No community can exist without such memories, and this is why it is so important for the Church to remember—in a parish, in a religious community, or in the Church as a whole. Beatifications and canonizations say something about the identity of a community that recalls its outstanding members. Remembering creates identity, creates the knowledge of where I belong. The worst thing that can happen to a group, a community, or a society is the loss of its shared memory, for then it has no future. It is rootless and homeless. Celebrations of remembrance are often rather stiff and formal, but we know how important it is to be reminded of our roots. The remembrance of the dead is a significant aspect of this collective memory.

There is surely no religion that emphasizes remembrance more strongly than Judaism. And this brings us back once more to the native soil of our Christian faith.

Perhaps this dimension is inherent in the mystery of the Jewish people. God chose this small people and gave it the immense task of bearing the promise of salvation for the whole world. This is why the Old Testament is full of exhortations to remember and not to forget: "Forget not all his benefits!" (Ps 103:2). No other people attaches so much importance to genealogies as the Jewish people. Where do I come from? Who are my ancestors? I have roots; I come from a long history that is ultimately woven together by God. The history of the Jewish people is told again and again. It is called to mind in our liturgy too—think of the readings in the Easter Vigil.

God is a God who acted. He chose this people and acted in its history. "Remember this day, in which you came out from Egypt, out of the house of bondage, for by strength of hand the LORD brought you out from this place" (Ex 13:3). For us too, this is the root of what we celebrate in the Eucharist.

Three times a day, the Jewish prayers include the words *Shema Israel,* "Hear, O Israel" (Deut 6:4). Hear and remember! The believing Jew and the Christian must always remember what God has done, and speak of his deeds "when you sit in your house, and when you walk by the way, and when you lie down, and when you rise. And you shall bind them as a sign upon your hand, and they shall be as frontlets between your eyes. And you shall write them on the doorposts of your house and on your gates" (Deut 6:7–9). Orthodox Jews take these words literally even today.

Remembrance is central to our liturgy too. The readings from the Old and New Testaments, the preface, and the eucharistic prayer are remembrances: What did God do? And above all, what did he do in Jesus?

The Past Becomes Present

In sacred scripture and the liturgy, remembrance is more than a mere act of recalling things from the past. It also involves making these realities present. The *Passover Haggadah* writes as follows about the Passover meal:

> Each one who now takes part in the celebration must consider himself as one who is now departing from Egypt, for it is written: "And you shall tell your son on that day, 'It is

because of what the LORD did for me when I came out of Egypt.' " It was not our ancestors alone that the Holy One, blessed be he, redeemed. He redeemed us too along with them, and this is why it is written: "He brought us too out of there, in order to bring us into the land that he had sworn to give to our ancestors."

At the *seder*, believing Jews say, "We too are departing from Egypt." And when we celebrate the Eucharist, we are basically doing exactly the same; we too are present in the upper room with Jesus and his disciples.

Sephardic Jews have a beautiful ritual. The father of the household stands up, takes the unleavened bread, wraps it in a cloth, and slings it over his shoulder; then he begins to walk in place, singing a song of departure. This shows clearly that we are not simply departing from Egypt in an act of remembering. We are departing from Egypt *now*, just like our ancestors.

At the *Magnificat* in Evening Prayer on Christmas Day, we sing the antiphon *Hodie Christus natus est*, "Today Christ has been born." At Pentecost, the *Magnificat* antiphon begins, "On this day the Holy Spirit appeared before the apostles in the tongues of fire . . ." This is a present reality. We are right in the heart of the event that we recall. On Holy Thursday, in the prayer over the gifts, we say, "Whenever the memorial of this sacrifice is celebrated the work of our redemption is accomplished." [1] The *Catechism of the Catholic Church* affirms:

---

[1] The same prayer is used on the Second Sunday in Ordinary Time; see also the Second Vatican Council, *Lumen Gentium* 3; *Catechism of the Catholic Church*, 2nd ed. (Vatican City: Libreria Editrice Vaticana; Washington, D.C.: United States Catholic Conference, 2000), 1364 (hereafter cited as *CCC*).

In the sense of sacred scripture the *memorial* is not merely the recollection of past events but the proclamation of the mighty works wrought by God for men (cf. Ex 13:3). In the liturgical celebration of these events, they become in a certain way present and real. This is how Israel understands its liberation from Egypt: every time Passover is celebrated, the Exodus events are made present to the memory of believers so that they may conform their lives to them.[2]

Recalling in a Double Sense

Accordingly, "Do this in memory of me" means, when you remember and celebrate in remembrance, it becomes a present reality. We could say that we are present in the upper room.

These words have yet another meaning. The criminal who was crucified at the right hand of Jesus said, "Jesus, remember me when you come into your kingdom" (Lk 23:42). This means, first of all, "Do not forget me! When you are 'on the other side', remember me and come to fetch me." God is often asked, "Remember our distress!" God does not forget his people. In the book of Exodus, when Moses had his decisive encounter at the burning bush, "The LORD said, 'I have seen the affliction of my people who are in Egypt, and have heard their cry because of their taskmasters; I know their sufferings, and I have come down to deliver them out of the hand of the Egyptians, and to bring them up out of that land to a good and broad land, a land flowing with milk and honey" (3:7–8). If only it were so today!

[2] *CCC* 1363; italics in original.

We pray insistently for peace in the land that God promised to his people. We pray that milk and honey may flow there instead of blood. God remembers his people.

In remembrance, there are two movements: we remember God, and God remembers us. "Do this in memory of me" means not only "Remember me", but also, "Remind God of me." And this is the second significant dimension of Jesus' words.

In the *Benedictus*, Zechariah prays, "He has remembered his holy covenant, the oath which he swore to our father Abraham" (Lk 1:72–73). God remembers his covenant.

When Jesus says, "Do this in remembrance of me", this also means, "Do this, so that God may remember me!" This sounds surprising. Why should we remind God of Jesus? One of the Psalms prays, "O Lord, remember David and all the hardships he endured" (132:1). Why must God remember David? The reason is very simple: "O God, restore again the kingdom of our father David!" (cf. Amos 9:11; Acts 1:6). Come to our aid! Do not forget us! When we remember Jesus in the Eucharist, we are praying to God that his kingdom may come. "Remember Jesus! Remember his promises! Remember the promises you have made!"

At the point where Jesus spoke the words over the cup, at the prayer of blessing over the third cup at the close of the Passover meal, the following prayer is spoken:

> Our God, God of our fathers, let the remembrance of us ascend to you, come to you, reach you, be seen by you, find acceptance by you, be heard by you, be considered by you, and be remembered by you, with the consideration of (our situation) and the remembrance of our fathers and the remembrance of the Messiah, the son of David your servant, and the remembrance of Jerusalem your holy city, and

the remembrance of your entire people, the house of Israel, before you—for redemption and favor.

This prayer certainly goes back to the time of Jesus, who probably spoke it himself. "Do this in memory of me" means, therefore, "Remind God of the promise that he gave through me!" Suddenly, we are no longer only in the past and the present but also in the future, because his words mean, "Do this, in order that his kingdom may come."

The Mass is thus already an anticipation of the glory that is to come. In every Mass, we pray, "Come, Lord Jesus!" This is an essential element in the Eucharist, but we are often insufficiently aware of it.

In the First Letter to the Corinthians, Paul writes about the Eucharist: "As often as you eat this bread and drink the chalice, you proclaim the Lord's death until he comes" (11:26). This is often understood (and translated): "until he comes again", but Saint Paul's words are more than an affirmation about something that will, in fact, happen in the future. They also mean, "you proclaim the Lord's death *so that* he may come again." This is a prayer full of longing. And this is why we say after the consecration, "We proclaim your Death, O Lord, ... *until you come again.*" This also means, "so that you may come again". Our wish is that you may come again.

The early Christians sang in every liturgy, *Maranatha*, "Come, Lord!" (cf. *Didache* 10.6). Down through the centuries, churches have been built facing east. We celebrate the Eucharist facing the dawning light, because we are on the watch in every Mass for the glory that is to come. We ought to be more conscious, when we celebrate the Mass, that the liturgy not only makes the Lord present but also longs for his future coming.

> By tradition, the Jews await the coming of Messiah in the middle of the night on which the Passover is celebrated, the night of the liberation from Egypt.... I believe that this is the origin of the apostolic tradition that the people may not be dismissed before midnight in the celebration of the Easter night, because they await the coming of Christ. And after this hour has passed, all celebrate the feast in the certainty of his coming.[3]

The Church Father Jerome (died 420) writes here about an ancient tradition whereby the faithful are not dismissed from the Easter Vigil before midnight. On this night, they await the coming of the Lord, wholly in keeping with the Jewish tradition that awaits the coming of the Messiah on this same night. The Easter Vigil of the early Christians did not end before midnight, because they awaited the second coming of the Lord on that night; and after midnight, they did not return home disappointed but celebrated the Eucharist, in which the Lord comes. He is hidden under the forms of bread and wine, but he is there in our midst.

"Do this in memory of me!" This means that we recall what the Lord did, and think of what is still to come. In the third eucharistic prayer, the priest says, "O Lord, as we celebrate the memorial of the saving Passion of your Son, his wondrous Resurrection and Ascension into heaven, and as we look forward to his second coming ..." This yearning for the return of the Lord is the driving force in the liturgy. Is it this same yearning that moves us to take part in the liturgy? It resounds at every point in the celebration: "The Lord be with you!" The Lord is coming to you! Receive him! In Holy Communion the Lord truly comes to us, hidden under the outward form of the sacrament.

---

[3] Jerome, *Commentary on Matthew* 4.25.6 (Patrologia latina 26:184).

The Eucharist in the Early Church

Would a second-century Christian feel at home in today's Mass? Would he realize that he is doing what Jesus told his disciples to do? He would find many things strange and confusing, and yet I am convinced that he would have the same experience that we have when for the first time we take part in the Orthodox liturgy. Everything seems foreign—the chants, the vestments, the rites—but when we look a little more closely and someone explains things to us, we see that all the elements of our own liturgy are there. They have a different form, but the basic structure is the same.

The New Testament itself tells us little about how the Eucharist was celebrated. All that we know is what the Acts of the Apostles tells us about the earliest Church: "They held steadfastly to the apostles' teaching and fellowship, to the breaking of the bread and to the prayers. . . . And day by day, attending the temple together and breaking bread in their homes, they partook of food with glad and generous hearts" (2:42, 46). It is certain that they celebrated the Eucharist on the first day of the week, and it seems highly likely that they did so every day.

It would be a good idea if we stopped speaking of the "weekend"—even if that is a difficult thing to ask. For Christians, Sunday is the first day of the week, and Saturday is the last day!

We have the good fortune to have an early description of the liturgy. Saint Justin, philosopher and martyr, wrote to the Roman emperor circa 155 in order to explain what Christians did:

On the day we call the day of the sun, all who dwell in the city or country gather in the same place. The memoirs of

the apostles and the writings of the prophets are read, as
much as time permits.

Here we have the Liturgy of the Word: the Old Testament,
the Gospels, and the Letters of the apostles.

When the reader has finished, he who presides over those
gathered admonishes and challenges them to imitate these
beautiful things.

Already at this early period, the presider—a bishop or a
priest—preached.

Then we all rise together and offer prayers for ourselves . . .
and for all others, wherever they may be, so that we may
be found righteous by our life and actions, and faithful to
the commandments, so as to obtain eternal salvation.

We too are familiar with these intercessions, which we call
the prayers of the faithful or bidding prayers.

When the prayers are concluded we exchange the kiss.

The sign of peace existed as early as circa 155. It still comes
at this place, after the intercessions, in the liturgy of the
Eastern churches; in the Latin rite, it comes immediately
before Communion.

Then someone brings bread and a cup of water and wine
mixed together to him who presides over the brethren. He
takes them and offers praise and glory to the Father of the
universe, through the name of the Son and of the Holy
Spirit, and for a considerable time he gives thanks [*eucharistia*] that we have been judged worthy of these gifts.

This is the eucharistic prayer.

When he has concluded the prayers and thanksgivings, all
present give voice to an acclamation by saying: "Amen."

When he who presides has given thanks and the people have responded, those whom we call deacons give to those present the "eucharisted" bread, wine and water and take them to those who are absent.[4]

This is Holy Communion. Another element with which we are familiar today was present even then.

Those who are well off, and who are also willing, give as each chooses. What is gathered is given to him who presides to assist orphans and widows, those whom illness or any other cause has deprived of resources, prisoners, immigrants, and, in a word, all who are in need.[5]

Justin concludes his account by saying that because this bread and wine have been made Eucharist (literally, "eucharisted"),

we call this food *Eucharist*, and no one may take part in it unless he believes that what we teach is true, has received baptism for the forgiveness of sins and new birth, and lives in keeping with what Christ taught.[6]

"Do this in memory of me!" This is how Justin describes the Mass circa 155, and we do this even today.

---

[4] Justin, *1 Apology* 65, 67; translation in *CCC* 1345.
[5] Ibid., 67.6; translation in *CCC* 1351.
[6] Ibid., 66.1–2; translation in *CCC* 1355; italics in original.

5

THE MASS—A SACRIFICE?

In what sense is the Eucharist a sacrifice? There are various ways to approach this question. In this book, I want to apply the following principle. If we want to know what the Church believes, then we must look at what she celebrates. A very ancient Christian aphorism states, *Lex orandi, lex credendi*, "The law of praying is also the law of the Church's faith", or as the *Catechism* puts it, "The Church believes as she prays." [1] When we ask in what sense the Mass is a sacrifice, we must therefore begin by looking at how the Church prays.

The Liturgy of the Church

Let us begin with a remark about the Church's celebration. It is fundamentally important that we do not attempt to present our own personal ideas in the Mass. We must celebrate the liturgy of the Church. This applies to the presider of the Eucharist (the priest and the bishop) but also to the liturgy committees in our parishes. Their job is not to stage experiments with the liturgy but to celebrate it worthily and in keeping with its innermost meaning. Sometimes the

[1] *CCC* 1124.

faithful are sorely tried by the excessively subjective caprices of the liturgical planners. Why must an entire parish be forced to accept the highly subjective—and sometimes wholly arbitrary—ideas of liturgical planners? Naturally, this applies above all to the Mass, which is the heart of the Church and the heart of her liturgical life. Here great reverence is needed.

On the other hand, this does not mean that the celebration of the Mass must be timid and rigid. We can relax, setting aside our own subjectivity and entering into the celebration of the liturgy. I see the liturgy as a mystagogy, an initiation into the mystery. When we let ourselves be led by the liturgy, the Church takes us by the hand, so to speak, and introduces us into the mystery of faith. This requires a great fidelity to the rite, that is, to the traditional shape of the liturgy, as well as a genuine willingness to let oneself be formed and shaped and deeply marked by the liturgy.

This truth always strikes me with particular intensity when I am present at the liturgy of the Eastern churches. The liturgy in our Latin rite is usually so short that there is hardly time to relax properly. An Eastern liturgy that lasts for two, two and a half, or even three hours makes it possible to get attuned to the Eucharist. The soul has the time it needs to enter into the celebration of the mystery. I believe that we have a lot to learn from the Eastern churches on this point.

Both the community and its priest must avoid the temptation of *celebrating their own selves*. Our task is not to celebrate a liturgy that will be as "original" as possible but to give *Christ* the space in which his word can be heard, so that his coming in the Eucharist will be genuinely the center of the rite. It is he who is the true celebrant. Bishops and priests are servants of Christ or, as Paul puts it, "stewards of the mysteries of God" (1 Cor 4:1). The community assembles not around the priest or around its own self but around Christ.

Sacrifice in the Third Eucharistic Prayer

Let us look for guidance to the celebration of the liturgy in our investigation of the sacrificial character of the Mass. In the not-so-distant past, it was perfectly natural to speak of "the holy sacrifice of the Mass", but this expression is not so familiar today. Let us look at the texts and ask to what extent we are justified in speaking of the Mass as a sacrifice. We shall read the third eucharistic prayer, which was newly formulated after the Second Vatican Council but consists in its entirety of elements drawn from the liturgy of the early Church.

It begins immediately after the Sanctus with the praise of God from the perspective of creation.

> You are indeed Holy, O Lord, and all you have created rightly gives you praise, for through your Son our Lord Jesus Christ, by the power and working of the Holy Spirit, you give life to all things and make them holy, and you never cease to gather a people to yourself, so that from the rising of the sun to its setting a pure sacrifice may be offered to your name.

This passage ends with a quotation from the prophet Malachi, who thunders against the superficial cult in the temple and announces a time to come when "a pure offering" will be made to God "from the rising of the sun to its setting ... among the nations" (1:11). The third eucharistic prayer thus states that this "pure sacrifice"—*oblatio munda* in Latin—is the Mass. The Eucharist is a sacrifice that is offered to the name of God at all times and places, from the rising of the sun to its setting. Malachi's prophecy also implies that there is only one sacrifice. Christ offered himself "once and for all" as the perfect sacrifice (cf. Heb 7:27; 9:12). There is *only one sacrifice*, through which he fulfilled all the sacrifices that have ever existed. What does this mean for the "sacrifice of the Mass"?

After the words of consecration comes the *anamnesis*, the act of remembering. The Church recalls the mighty deeds of God, especially those connected with Jesus Christ:

> O Lord, as we celebrate the memorial of the saving Passion of your Son, his wondrous Resurrection and Ascension into heaven, and as we look forward to his second coming, we offer you in thanksgiving this holy and living sacrifice.

Christ offered sacrifice once and for all, but this prayer affirms that "we offer" sacrifice. What is this "holy and living sacrifice" that we "offer"?

> Look, we pray, upon the oblation of your Church and, recognizing the sacrificial Victim by whose death you willed to reconcile us to yourself . . .

The third canon speaks once again of the Church's sacrifice (Latin: *oblationem Ecclesiae tuae*). This sacrifice is Christ, the Lamb who was slain in sacrifice. The Latin text reads *agnoscens hostiam cuius voluisti immolatione placari*, literally, "recognizing the Victim by whose immolation you willed to be reconciled . . ."

> May he make of us an eternal offering to you.

We ourselves are to become a sacrifice. The Latin text reads *Ipse nos tibi perficiat munus aeternum*, literally, "May he make us an everlasting sacrificial gift to you." We see, therefore, that the third canon speaks first of the sacrifice of Christ, then of the sacrifice offered by the Church, and third of the sacrifice that we ourselves must become. This is summed up in the following powerful words:

> May this Sacrifice of our reconciliation, we pray, O Lord, advance the peace and salvation of all the world.

This shows the tremendous power of the Eucharist: it brings *peace and salvation to the entire world.* Only two alternatives are possible. Either these words are an appalling exaggeration, or else this sacrifice truly possesses an unimaginable power. What is "this Sacrifice of our reconciliation"? Is it the sacrifice of Christ, the sacrifice of the Mass, or the gift that we make of our own selves? The text speaks only of "this Sacrifice".

Naturally, the other eucharistic prayers likewise speak of sacrifice: of the sacrifice of Christ, the sacrifice of the Church, and the sacrifice that each of us is called to become. And this sacrifice—embracing all these dimensions—will bring the entire world peace and salvation.

Several Questions about Sacrifice

Many questions arise here. What is a sacrifice? What does it mean to offer a sacrifice? Does God demand sacrifices?

Many abuses are possible here. A sacrificial attitude can be a pretext for evading problems. Instead of endeavoring to solve the problems, one "makes sacrifices". Adopting a sacrificial attitude can thus be a way to avoid taking action that could change one's situation. It can also be an expression of self-righteousness: "Look at what I am doing! Look at the sacrifices I am making! See how I am sacrificing myself for you!" There is certainly a danger that mothers (and sometimes fathers too) can use their devotion to apply emotional pressure to their families: "Look at all I do for you! What do you do for me?" This can take the extreme form of blackmail: "I sacrifice myself for you, and you don't love me . . ." In such relationships, sacrifice seems an expression of a refusal to live, or indeed of a fear of life itself. Such psychological objections are well known. Instead of adopting the victim's role, I ought to become active and *do* something.

There are also very weighty theological objections to sacrifice. Do we not find on the lips of Christ himself polemic against sacrifices? Did he not make it very clear that mercy is much more important than all sacrifices (Mt 9:13; 12:7; Hos 6:6)? What effect can sacrifice have if love is lacking? Did not Jesus replace the sacrifices of the old covenant with the commandment of love? Another theological objection argues that if the death of Christ is indeed a sacrifice, then it is the only sacrifice, offered once and for all (Heb 7:27); and this means that we need no new sacrifices—and no "sacrifice of the Mass".

The Reformation polemic vigorously attacked the sacrifice of the Mass and the various customs associated with this idea. For example, the faithful would ask for the celebration of a sequence of thirty Masses, one after another, the so-called Gregorian Masses. People in the Middle Ages were profoundly convinced of the efficacy of the sacrifice of the Mass, especially for the dead, and this is why so many requests were made for Masses to be celebrated. In my young days, it was still very normal to give priests a stipend to have Masses celebrated for the dead, but nowadays I find myself rather embarrassed when bishops from poor countries write to me and ask, "Have you any Mass stipends for us? Our priests have no income other than these Mass stipends." I have to tell them that Catholics in Austria today give far fewer stipends.

The Reformation criticized this praxis; and there were, of course, many abuses at that time. Indulgences too were linked to the sacrifice of the Mass, and some of the Protestant criticism was perfectly justified. From today's perspective, however, we must say that some of this criticism was not at all justified.

Martin Luther (died 1546) fought vehemently against the doctrine of the eucharistic sacrifice, which he called "almost the worst of all abuses", since "almost all the world has now turned the Mass into a sacrifice." [2] Let me quote some of his words. Luther—like the Catholic controversialists of the sixteenth century—used strong language. He called the sacrifice of the Mass a "dragon's penis" that "begot much vermin and dung and much idolatry".[3] And when the possibility of reunion between Catholics and Protestants was discussed, Luther stated very clearly that on this question "we are and remain forever divided and opposed to one another. They understand very well that if the Mass falls, the papacy too will lie on the ground in ruins." [4] Luther believed that he was *obliged* to abandon the idea of the eucharistic sacrifice. His style may be aggressive, but this was not just cheap polemic. He was profoundly convinced that we are not redeemed by human work. It is God who has redeemed us. The sacrifice of Christ is God's work, not a human work, and the idea that *we* share in the sacrifice of Christ and can ourselves contribute something to it would eliminate an essential element of what Luther saw as the core of the Christian faith. He regarded the sacrifice of the

[2] *D. Martin Luthers Werke: Kritische Gesamtausgabe* [Weimarer Ausgabe] (Weimar: H. Böhlaus Nachfolger, 1883–), 6:365.

[3] Ibid., 50:204.

[4] Ibid.; cf. W. Averbeck, *Der Opfercharakter des Abendmahls* [The sacrificial character of the Lord's Supper] (Paderborn, 1967), p. 33.

Mass as a human work and saw it as encouraging human self-righteousness.

Even today, the question of the eucharistic sacrifice leads us into the heart of our faith. Is this something done by human beings, an "achievement" for which we can congratulate ourselves? Does the sacrifice make the work of God superfluous? Must we offer God sacrifices? Does God need this? Is not God infinitely greater than all our sacrifices could ever be?

Finally, many people today ask, "Did Jesus himself offer a sacrifice?" We have just heard the words of the third eucharistic prayer: "Look, we pray, upon the oblation of your Church"—*oblationem Ecclesiae tuae*—"and, recognizing the sacrificial Victim by whose death you willed to reconcile us to yourself . . ." What kind of God lets himself be reconciled to mankind by a sacrifice?

And so the question remains: Does God need sacrifices?

Multiple Meanings of the Word "Sacrifice"

The German word *Opfer* can be translated both as "sacrifice" and as "victim". It is a word in common use, but what does it mean? Let me give some examples from everyday life. I hope that tomorrow's newspapers will not speak of new *victims of terrorism*. We hear of *victims of traffic accidents*. This word tells us that someone has been hurt. It denotes violence—we speak of *victims of sexual abuse*, making a distinction between *the one who suffers* and *the one who inflicts the suffering*. A victim is one who suffers violence that affects him very deeply, or even destroys his life.

The Bible uses the word "sacrifice" in another context, which is also reflected in our everyday language. When something is costly, we can call it a sacrifice. When you come into this cold cathedral to hear my catecheses, instead of sitting comfortably at home, that is a sacrifice that requires willpower! When you put money into the collection in church on Sunday, that too could be called a sacrifice. Sacrifices are costly; we have to overcome our own inner resistance. And this is why the word also has negative overtones.

An old friend once told me that she had to take piano lessons as a child and hated it. When she was fourteen years old, however, she began to enjoy playing the piano; but then her grandmother, a strict puritan, made her stop, because it was forbidden to do anything that gave one pleasure. Here, "sacrifice" is an exclusively negative reality.

We may therefore be surprised when we look at the Christian tradition. It was Saint Augustine (died 430) who offered the classic definition of "sacrifice" in the West (although his words were often forgotten down through the ages): "What is a true sacrifice? It is every work that helps us to adhere to God in a holy community." [5] This is a wide and open definition of sacrifice. The core is the establishing of a community. Sacrifice, in the religious sense of this word, unites us in *sancta societate*, a "holy community", with God. This is why praise is a sacrifice, and the book of Psalms speaks of the "sacrifice of praise" (50:23) because praise creates community between us and God. This is why scripture also calls meals sacrifices, because a sacred meal creates community with God and with other people.

This too can be costly. Where there are obstacles to the establishing of this community, I must make a sacrifice of reconciliation. This, however, is not the essence of sacrifice. The effort of overcoming myself, the small daily sacrifice of attentiveness, kindness, smiling, listening to others,

[5] *City of God* 10.6.

giving others my time—all this creates community, and the effort involved can actually bring joy. The essence of sacrifice is the creation of community. This sheds a new light on the question posed above. It is not God who needs sacrifice. It is we who need it, so that we can enter again and again into community with him.

Let us look once again at what the Bible has to say about the essence of sacrifice. In Psalm 51, the great penitential psalm, we read, "The sacrifice acceptable to God is a broken spirit; a broken and contrite heart, O God, you will not despise" (51:17). A spirit that returns to God is the true sacrifice; the external sacrifices are not so important. Jesus says, "I desire mercy, and not sacrifice" (Mt 9:13; 12:7; cf. Hos 6:6). Why is mercy the true sacrifice that Jesus seeks? The answer is simple: because it creates community.

The Eucharist as Memorial of the Sacrifice of Christ

At the beginning of the third eucharistic prayer, we hear the words "so that from the rising of the sun to its setting a pure sacrifice may be offered to your name." We believe that the Eucharist is this pure sacrifice, but what exactly does this mean? *Is* the Eucharist a sacrifice?

Let us look at what happens in the Mass. We have what might be called a sacrificial procession in which the gifts, especially bread and wine, are brought to the altar; in solemn liturgies, this procession is particularly elaborate. I have experienced this very vividly in Africa, where whole sacks of manioc, fruits, and a live goat—a sign of special honor for the guest from Vienna—as well as hens were brought to the altar. The high point was a live calf! We call this part of the liturgy the offertory, the preparation of the gifts. Bread and wine are offered, and if we listen attentively, we learn that it is we ourselves who are the gift: "May he make of *us* an eternal offering to you." Our contribution is our own selves. But above all, the sacrificial gift is the Body and Blood of the Lord himself.

Can we offer to God in sacrifice bread and wine, changed into the Body and Blood of Christ? Is it not rather the case that the Father makes a gift to us, that God is the author of this gift? Are we permitted in the Mass to give Christ back to God as a gift? Well, this is as a matter of fact how the Church understands her prayer. No matter how the ecumenical dialogue may develop, the basic meaning of the liturgy is clear: the Church believes that she offers Christ in sacrifice to the Father.

But does not this supersede the unique sacrifice that Christ offered? Is the holy sacrifice of the Mass a new sacrifice? If we consult the *Catechism*, we find that the Eucharist is indeed a sacrifice; but it is a sacrifice because it is the memorial of the sacrifice of Christ.[6] Memorial and sacrifice are intimately linked. The third canon prays, "O Lord, as we celebrate the memorial of the saving Passion of your Son ... we offer you in thanksgiving this holy and living sacrifice." In Latin, this sentence begins, *Memores igitur offerimus*, literally, "Being mindful, therefore, we offer ..." *Because* we recall the sacrifice of Christ in the Mass, this sacrifice becomes present.

We have seen above that when we recall the Last Supper of Jesus and his death, we are present at these events. This is why the *Catechism* goes on to say, "The sacrifice of Christ and the sacrifice of the Eucharist are *one single sacrifice*"— then and now. The text continues, quoting the Council of Trent, "The victim is one and the same: the same now offers

---

[6] *CCC* 1365–66.

through the ministry of priests, who then offered himself on the cross; only the manner of offering is different": then it was bloody, today it is unbloody.[7]

The Eucharist is a sacrifice of the Church—how are we to understand this? The *Catechism* answers, "The Church which is the Body of Christ participates in the offering of her Head. With him, she herself is offered whole and entire."[8] The Church and Christ are one. When Christ offers himself as a gift to the Father for all mankind, the Church offers herself as a gift along with him.

In his *Sermon* 272, Saint Augustine expressed this truth in words that have never been surpassed:

> If then you are the Body of Christ and his members, it is your own mystery that is set down upon the table of the Lord. You receive your own mystery and you answer "Amen" to what you yourselves are. . . . For you hear the words: "The Body of Christ", and you answer: "Amen." Be a member of Christ, in order that your "Amen" may be true. . . . Hear what the apostle says: "We who are many are one bread, one Body" [1 Cor 10:17]. Understand this, and rejoice! . . . One bread! Who is this "one bread"? The many are one bread! Recall that one does not make bread from one grain of wheat, but from many! You have been exorcised [in baptism], and on that occasion you were ground, so to speak. When you were baptized, you were in a sense kneaded. And when you received the fire of the Holy Spirit, you were in a sense baked.

Now you are the body of Christ, the bread of Christ. Augustine continues: "Be therefore what you see, and receive what you are."

---

[7] *CCC* 1367; italics in original.
[8] *CCC* 1368.

6

THE CONSECRATION

Once when I was in the United States, I met a man who suffered from multiple sclerosis and was confined to a wheelchair. In addition, he suffered from celiac disease, in which the gluten in wheat makes the immune system produce antibodies that attack the body's own tissues. This means that one cannot consume normal Hosts, since these are made of wheat flour. The Congregation for the Doctrine of the Faith has studied this matter and has approved the use of gluten-free Hosts for sufferers of celiac disease. I told this man, "You could receive Communion with gluten-free Hosts." But he replied, "I do not eat bread. But I do receive the Body of Christ." In other words, he accepted the risk to his health entailed by receiving a normal Host. This answer surprised me, and I certainly would not recommend other sufferers of celiac disease to imitate him. At the same time, however, this convinced Catholic was bearing testimony to the logic of his own faith in a way that impressed me.

This brings us to the central question of the present chapter: Why do we say *the Body of Christ* rather than *the bread of Christ*?

Preliminary Comments: Bread and the Body of Christ

After the words of institution, the priest genuflects. If there were merely a piece of bread on the altar, this gesture would be meaningless. No doubt, we should regard every piece of bread with reverence, and we should not simply throw it thoughtlessly away. But no one genuflects in front of a piece of bread. I bow down before God in person. The bodily gesture expresses the fact that Jesus Christ is present under the form of bread.

We all know that what we see, taste, and touch is bread. If we were to examine the Host under an electron microscope, we would not be able to discern any change that had been brought about by the words of consecration. It remains bread. And yet we say "the Body of Christ".

There is undeniably a great tension between the palpable outward reality and the words that we use. How do we deal with this tension, for example, when we prepare children for their First Holy Communion? It is, of course, important to help the children grasp the symbolism of bread, since we live in an age in which bread seems to have lost virtually all its value—and this means that it is helpful to have the children bake bread in the course of their sacramental preparation. But how do we take the step beyond the bread to the Body of Christ?

One of my great cares as bishop is the way we deal with the eucharistic gifts. Are we all truly aware, when we receive Communion, that this is the Body of the Lord? Often, people in the German-speaking regions speak only of *geweihtes Brot*, literally, "blessed bread", but this is highly misleading, since there is a completely different reality that already has this name. This blessed bread (*eulogia* in Greek) is distributed at the end of the liturgy of the Eucharist in the Eastern

Church. It is not Holy Communion; it is a tiny survival of
the *agape*, the meal that was held after the liturgy in the
early Church. We Catholics do not receive Communion in
the Orthodox service, since the Orthodox Churches do not
permit this, and we respect their point of view; but we are
allowed to share the "blessed bread" with them. The Eucharist itself is something essentially different: it is the Body of
Christ and his Blood.

The consecration is the innermost mystery of the Eucharist. When we approach the consecration, two mistaken attitudes are possible.

One attitude could be compared to the attitude that Moses
takes at the burning bush. He is in the wilderness with the
flock of his father-in-law, Jethro, when he suddenly sees a
thornbush that is burning but is not consumed. His curi-
osity is awakened, and he says, "I will turn aside and see
this great sight, why the bush is not burnt." He approaches
the bush, but God's voice addresses him, "Do not come
near; put off your shoes from your feet, for the place on
which you are standing is holy ground." And Moses hides
his face (Ex 3:1–6). In the parish church of Schruns in western Austria where I grew up, the burning bush is depicted
immediately above the altar. As a child, I often looked at
this picture, but I did not know why it was there. Later, I
understood that those who painted the walls of this neo-
Romanesque church in the nineteenth century were guided
by a very precise idea: the proper location for the picture of
the burning bush is above the altar, since it symbolizes the
incomprehensible mystery of the Eucharist. If one becomes
curious and attempts to penetrate the mystery, wondering
what it is, one hears the words of the liturgy: it is the *mystery* of faith. We do not take off our shoes, nor do we veil
our faces, but many people kneel down or seek to adopt

some other bodily posture that expresses veneration, adoration, and faith. At all costs, we must not look directly at the Host. For if we really grasped what takes place at the consecration, our terror—and our joy—would be so intolerable that we would die on the spot.

The second possible mistaken attitude would be to say, "You must believe, but you must not ask any questions." This too is an un-Christian attitude. We are allowed to ask questions. Faith seeks to understand, just as love seeks to understand.

This must, however, be a reverent asking, not a rationalism. In the late Middle Ages, the so-called nominalists often took a one-sidedly intellectual pleasure in posing questions. The Pilgram pulpit in Saint Stephen's Cathedral bears witness to this. It portrays the four Latin Church Fathers, and we see Pope Gregory the Great (died 604) holding a Host in his hand and looking highly skeptical. I may be doing Master Anton Pilgram (or whoever actually sculpted the pulpit) an injustice, but I find the figure of Saint Gregory disturbing: it is hard to accept that someone with that particular expression on his face really believes in what he is holding in his hand. At the end of the sixteenth century, there were so many hairsplitting scholastic questions that faith was often left stranded by the wayside, and we can grasp why Martin Luther, one generation later, said, "Enough discussion! We must believe! *Sola fides*, faith alone!"

The Two Lungs of the Church

Blessed John Paul II often said that the Church breathes with two lungs, the Eastern and the Western. The Christian East and the Christian West have developed two specific ways of approaching the mystery of the consecration.

The Christian East takes its primary starting point for contemplation of the mystery of the consecration in the mystery of the Incarnation. Just as God has become man, so Christ becomes the Eucharist. Just as Mary was overshadowed by the Holy Spirit and conceived Christ, so the Holy Spirit descends on the bread and wine and transforms them into the Body and Blood of Christ. This is why the invocation of the Holy Spirit is so important in the Christian East. In the liturgy of the Russian, Greek, and other Orthodox churches, the celebrant of the Eucharist prostrates himself on the ground at the moment when he invokes the descent of the Holy Spirit upon the gifts of bread and wine. Just as Mary conceived by the Holy Spirit, so the power of the Holy Spirit takes hold of these gifts of bread and wine and transforms them.

The Church's Western lung, the Latin tradition, as represented in the Catholic liturgy, takes a somewhat different approach. Its starting point tends to be the creative Word of God. Just as God the Creator made all things through his mighty Word, so this same Word transforms bread and wine into the Body and Blood of Christ. This is why the words of consecration play such an important role in our liturgy. They are the most solemn moment in the Mass. When the priest or bishop speaks the words of consecration, it is the creative power of the word of Christ himself, who is himself the Word of God, that brings about the transformation.

Let us proceed in three steps. First, I shall look at the Eastern approach to the mystery, and second, I shall consider how this mystery is viewed in the Christian West, in the Latin Church. Third, I shall look over the shoulder of Saint Thomas Aquinas (died 1274) in his atelier, so to speak, and ask how the great doctor of the Eucharist seeks to open a path into the heart of this mystery. It was Thomas who composed the liturgical texts and hymns that we sing even today on the feast of Corpus Christi.

The East: Incarnation and Eucharist

Let us begin by looking at the Eastern lung. We can call the Eastern tradition "Johannine", since we find in the Gospel of John the embodiment of what the Christian East has to say to us.

Our starting point is the great discourse about the bread of life that has come down from heaven. Jesus presents a tremendous vision to his hearers in the synagogue at Capernaum, who certainly found it very hard to accept these deep and powerful words. He says, "The bread of God is that which comes down from heaven, and gives life to the world. . . . I am the bread of life. . . . I am the living bread which came down from heaven" (Jn 6:33, 35, 51). These words offer us an approach to the mystery of the Eucharist. Jesus himself, and his entire life, is the bread from which people can live; he is food, and this is the very reason why he came into this world. There is a structural parallel between his becoming flesh and his becoming Eucharist, and this allows him to use the Eucharist to explain the purpose of his Incarnation.

The Gospel of John contains no speculative eucharistic theology; indeed, it contains no theological theories of any kind. Its concern is us and our salvation, and this is why Jesus goes one step further and says, "He who eats my flesh and drinks my blood abides in me, and I in him" (6:56). He himself is the bread of God, and we are to eat him in order that we may draw life from him.

People even then asked whether such words made any
sense. Can one really eat his flesh and drink his blood? "The
Jews disputed among themselves, saying, 'How can this man
give us his flesh to eat?'" (6:52). And many since then have
asserted that all this is meant to be understood "spiritually". In other words, we are moving on a symbolic level,
and what Jesus is really talking about is faith. After all, he
himself says, "He who believes has eternal life" (6:47).
Accordingly, when Jesus declares, "I am the bread of life",
he is exhorting us to believe. We might perhaps say that
whoever believes Jesus, "eats" him . . .

The evangelist John, however, employs a very concrete
word here. Our biblical translations read "He who *eats* my
flesh", but a literal translation would be "He who *bites* my
flesh"—that is, truly eats it!—"and drinks my blood has
eternal life" (6:54). And it is in *this* context that he says,
"He who believes has eternal life."

Jesus says that we are to drink his Blood. I have already
said how shocking this must have sounded in Jewish ears,
since Jews were forbidden to consume blood. And so the
objection is made: Do not Jesus' words here refer simply to
believing, in the sense that whoever believes has communion with Jesus? Once again, however, we must refuse the
"either-or". Yes, it is a question of believing, but it is also
a question of the Flesh and Blood of Jesus. With these words
of Jesus in mind, an early Church Father, Saint Ignatius of
Antioch (died before 117), wrote that those who reject this
teaching "stay away from the Eucharist and the prayer,
because they do not profess that the Eucharist is the flesh
of our Redeemer Jesus Christ, who suffered for our sins." [1]
It is good to listen to what the earliest Christians have to

[1] *Letter to the Smyrnaeans* 7.1.

tell us about how they understood the Eucharist. Around the year 100, this bishop and martyr was convinced that Jesus wanted us truly to eat his Flesh and drink his Blood.

But how do we do this? At the Last Supper, Jesus did not give the apostles a piece of flesh and a cup containing blood, but bread and the cup of wine. And yet he says that we are to eat his Flesh and drink his Blood.

People in the Roman Empire often laughed at the Christians, calling them "cannibals" who ate human flesh and drank human blood. (Later, unfortunately, medieval Christians turned this polemic against Jews, who were falsely accused of killing Christian children and drinking their blood.) Around the year 150, Justin Martyr gave the emperor the following account of what the Christians actually did:

> We do not receive it [that is, the Eucharist] as ordinary food and ordinary drink. Rather, just as Jesus Christ our Redeemer became flesh through the Word of God and took on flesh and blood for our redemption, so too our teaching affirms that the food that has become the Eucharist through the prayer of his Word is the flesh and blood of the Jesus who became flesh.[2]

As with the Incarnation, so with the Eucharist. The Word of God became flesh, and through the same Word and the same Spirit this food becomes the Body and Blood of Christ. We do not know whether the emperor actually read Justin's *apologia*, but if he did, he must have found it very difficult to understand the strange views held by the Christians. This is why Justin adds one further explanation: "as our flesh and blood are formed by the *transmutation* of what we eat".[3] When we eat, the food is transmuted into our own body.

---

[2] *1 Apology* 66.
[3] Ibid.

This is Justin's attempt at an explanation of how a trans-mutation makes natural food become the Body and Blood of Christ.

How are we to understand this transmutation? Justin uses the Greek word *metabolē*, from which the medical term "metabolism" is derived. Bread and wine are transformed into the Body and Blood of Christ. In order to make this at least a little more comprehensible to the emperor and to the pagans who read his *apologia*, he refers to the natural process of nutrition. "Look at the bread and the chalice of wine. Before the prayers and invocations are uttered, they are nothing more than bread and wine. . . . But when the great prayers and sacred invocations are sent up, the Logos descends into the bread and the chalice, and it becomes his Body." [4] What happens to the bread and wine when the Logos, the Word of God, descends upon this bread, as the Fathers say? In ancient Greek, the word *metabolismus* comes from the financial world and denotes the profit made in transfers of money. This was used as a metaphor to help explain how this bread is trans-ferred from its natural context to a new context; it becomes Christ's own possession, and he takes hold of it—or, as the early Christian catechesis of Saint Cyril of Jerusalem (died 386) puts it, the Holy Spirit is invoked "so that he may make the bread into the Body of Christ and the wine into the Blood of Christ; for everything that the Holy Spirit takes hold of is consecrated and transformed." [5] The Holy Spirit expropriates the bread, so to speak, and makes it into the Body of Christ. Bread and wine lose their natural autonomy and become the possession of Christ. They become his Body

---

[4] Attributed to Athanasius of Alexandria (died 373), fragment 7 (Patrolo-gia graeca 26:1325C).

[5] *Mystagogical Catecheses* 5.7.

and Blood. This does not *explain* the mystery, of course, but it is at any rate an attempt at an approach.

The West: God's Word Transforms Everything

Let us look at the Church's other wing, the Western tradition. Carlo Maria Cardinal Martini, the former archbishop of Milan, is a great catechist, but one of his early predecessors is even more celebrated, namely, Saint Ambrose (died 397), one of the most important exegetes and catechists in the Church's history. In his discourse to the newly baptized, who had received Holy Communion for the first time after their baptism on Easter night, he explains to them what they have received: "Perhaps you might wish to object: 'I see something else there—so how can you say to me that I am receiving the body of Christ?'"[6] The newly baptized person who puts such a question identifies very precisely the tension that characterizes the Christian faith up to the present day: I see bread, but I believe that this is the Body of Christ.

Saint Ambrose continues: Look at the Bible and see how many times the power of God's Word changes and transforms something. For example, God the Creator transforms with his power Moses' staff into a serpent and responds to Elijah's prayer by sending fire from heaven upon the sacrifice. This is even clearer in the miracles of Jesus, who simply says one word—and effects a healing. If the Word of God has such power, must it not be even easier for the mighty Word of God to transform something that already exists than to create it out of nothing? If God created

[6] *On the Mysteries* 9.50.

everything out of nothing, then his power is also able to change bread into the Body of Christ.[7]

Ambrose expresses this mystery by means of a word with which we are very familiar, *conversio*, "transformation".[8] This noun also means "conversion". Something fundamental has happened to the bread and wine; they are converted, transformed. Just as Paul calls the baptized "a new creation" (2 Cor 5:17), so the bread and wine are transformed by the Word of God into a new reality.

We have now seen two possible approaches to the mystery of the eucharistic consecration, although this does not mean that we have now understood it! On the one hand, we have seen that just as the Holy Spirit descends on Mary and she conceives the Son of God in her womb, so the bread is transformed into the Body of Christ through the power of the Holy Spirit. The other line says, since God's mighty Word created all things, it can also transform all things.

Thomas Aquinas: Transformation of the Essence

The basic question is: How real is this transformation? Does it take place in my own mind, in my imagination? Does it take place in faith? Or does a new reality come into existence? But if it does take place in reality, why do we not see anything of this change? Where then does this transformation take place? What kind of a transformation is this? And what is it that actually changes? When we look back over the history of Western thought, we can see that this

[7] Ibid., 9.52; *On the Sacraments* 4.19–20.
[8] *On the Sacraments* 4.23.

question generated very profound reflections on reality, essence, the substance of matter, and transformations in matter and reality. For centuries, the West reflected intensely on this question of transformation, and we cannot trace every step along this path here.

I would, however, like to take you briefly with me into the atelier of Saint Thomas. Let me warn you in advance that the atmosphere there is rather dry. At first sight, there is nothing exciting there. But it becomes exciting once we start to think along the same lines as Thomas. For although everything appears technical, and what we see are the instruments of intellectual precision, we soon perceive, despite the sobriety of his language, that this great thinker had a heart burning with love.

Let us begin with the affirmation that bread remains bread—it looks like bread, and it tastes like bread—but we believe that it is the Body of Christ that is on the altar.

Medieval Christians asked a question at this point in their reflections: If it is the Body of Christ that is on the altar, and many Masses are celebrated (in those days, many Masses were celebrated simultaneously at the side altars of a church), then it follows that the Body of Christ must be continuously growing. However, this conclusion cannot be true!

Another question: What happens when Christ descends upon the altar and becomes present here? Does this mean that he leaves heaven? And if he is here, at this particular place, can he be somewhere else at the same time?

We may laugh at such questions, but they generated a heated discussion that lasted for centuries, and it was over this question that Martin Luther and John Calvin (died 1564) parted company. If Christ is in heaven right now, is it possible for him to descend upon our altars? Would that not mean that the Body of Christ was divided? And if the bread

is transformed into the Body of Christ and we break it,
does this mean that the Body of Christ is broken? Such
considerations led John Calvin and many other Reformers
to argue that it is more meaningful to affirm that the bread
remains bread but is a sign that reminds us of Christ. The
sign of bread raises our faith up to Christ, and when I believe,
I am united to him. Does not this seem more dignified
than the idea that the bread truly becomes the Body of
Christ? Martin Luther did not share this doctrine—and the
Catholic Church has completely rejected it.

Saint Thomas begins with an observation that is familiar
to us: we cannot grasp with our senses that Christ is in this
sacrament. This can be perceived *sola fide*, "by faith alone"—a
term that Martin Luther was later to use so often. But is it
meaningful to believe this? Thomas is convinced that it would
be inhuman to believe something that does not make sense.
Neither the Church nor Christ himself can force me to
believe something that is utterly absurd. Why then do we
find it meaningful to believe that the bread truly becomes
the Body of Christ, and the wine truly becomes his Blood?

I mention only one of the reasons that Thomas gives,
because I find myself in profound agreement with him. Jesus
wanted to show us his friendship, and this is not something
you show by being far distant but by being with your friends
as often as possible. Friends want to spend time in one
another's company. As far as our eyes are concerned, Jesus
has left us; but he wants to remain with us as our friend,
and this is why he has found this way of being with us.[9]

The true Body of Christ is in this sacrament, but one
does not see it. How does something enter a place where it
had not previously been? There are two possible answers to

---

[9] Thomas Aquinas, *Summa theologica* III, q. 75, art. 1.

this simple question. Saint Thomas offers an example: How does the fire come into a house when it begins to burn? One possibility is that the fire comes from outside, as happened in 1945 here in Vienna when sparks carried the fire to the roof of Saint Stephen's Cathedral and the entire building began to burn. Another possibility is that the house itself catches fire and thus transforms the wood into fire. Thomas then argues: When Jesus comes onto the altar, he does not do so by first leaving heaven in order to reach us. Jesus' presence with us is not a localized presence of that kind. He is not here in the way that we are here, localized in our bodies. Jesus comes by means of a transformation: the bread is transformed into his Body.

How can such a transformation take place? Look at what we ourselves do. If I take a handful of clay, I can form out of it a vase or a statue. At the same time, all I can do is to alter the *shape* of the clay. Another example will make the point clearer. When a child is educated by its parents, something in the child is transformed and develops; at the same time, if the child is not in fact a genius, the final result will not be a Mozart or an Einstein. The child can become only something in keeping with his inherent potential. All the transformations that we can recognize and observe are transformations of something that already exists. The same is true of the transformations in our own selves. Once I was a child and now I am older, but despite many changes, I am still the same. In the technical language of his atelier, Saint Thomas says that what we are observing here are "transformations of form".

Now comes the decisive term! These changes are not "transformations of substance", since the substance remains identical. The little child and the old man are the same human being. In our external environment, in the world

that we experience, we do not see transformations of substance. Thomas says that this is because we have only the
power to change something or to shape something but not
to create a substance anew. Only God can change the substance, since he can reach into the innermost dimension of
reality. He can create the world out of nothing, and he can
change bread into his Body. This led the Church to create
a term that belongs to the vocabulary of the faith (although
Thomas himself uses it seldom): the consecration in the Mass
is a *transubstantiation*.

It is difficult to understand these ideas. But it is not strictly
necessary for faith to do so. Thomas' arguments are an attempt
at an intellectual approach to the wonderful mystery whereby
Jesus becomes truly present, so that the bread is no longer
bread but becomes the Body of Christ, and the wine becomes
his Blood. Thomas calls this "transubstantiation", adding at
once that this is a mystery of faith. He then says—almost
with a sigh of relief—that it is in fact harder, for a variety of
reasons, to understand this transformation than to understand the creation itself.[10]

Conclusions: Importance for the Faith

Saint Thomas was a man of intense intellectual reflection,
and we have just paid a brief visit to his atelier. His final
word is the simple *Adoro te devote, latens Deitas*, "I adore
you devoutly, hidden Godhead." His seeking and his wonder bring him to adoration.

Let me finish by indicating three reasons why this mystery of the consecration is so important for our faith.

[10] Ibid., art. 4.

First, the eucharistic consecration strengthens our *faith* that the word of Christ and his Spirit are so powerful that he can transform sinners into righteous persons, people who are lost into people who are saved, and human beings into children of God. Each time I repeat "Lord, I believe that this is your Body and your Blood", my faith in the working of God increases.

Second, the eucharistic consecration strengthens our *hope* that the little piece of bread, the fruit of the earth, and the wine, the fruit of the vine and work of human hands, are transformed and become the beginning of a new world. One day, God will transform all things. He will wipe away all tears and make all things new. There will be a new heaven and a new earth. In this consecration, God gives us in effect the beginning of the new creation, and this is a great source of hope.

Third, the eucharistic consecration strengthens our *love*. Christ wishes to give himself to us so intimately that he becomes our food. He makes use of the forms of bread and wine in order to give his own self. In doing so, he strengthens our love of him who has the power to transform us, and he gives us the hope that we ourselves will also be transformed.

7

THE PRESENCE OF JESUS CHRIST
IN THE EUCHARIST

We believe that the Lord is present in the Eucharist. This certainty is expressed in many forms, for example, when we genuflect before the Blessed Sacrament, and it is central to every aspect of the Eucharist. But what kind of presence is this?

> Lord, in your love you wanted to be with us always. You give us your presence in the mystery of the Eucharist as a pledge of the glory that is to come. Let us grasp with the heart, with the understanding, and with faith the gift that your love gives us in this mystery. Amen.

"He Is There"

I begin by recalling Saint John Mary Vianney, the parish priest of Ars (died 1859), who was a great adorer of the eucharistic presence. He turned his back on his hearers again and again in the course of his catecheses, so that he faced the tabernacle, and he said simply, "*Il est là*. He is there!" Faith knows what these words mean, even if they remain inaccessible to reason.

Let me mention one other testimony, from the autobiography of Sister Miriam Prager, a Benedictine nun of Jewish origins in the convent of Saint Gabriel in Bertelstein.[1] She had grown up without any religious faith in a secularized Jewish environment. She was a young teacher under the celebrated pedagogue Maria Montessori in Belgium, and one day she went into the chapel of the nuns. She did not know what was taking place; all she grasped was that it was some kind of worship. And suddenly she knew with absolute certainty, "I must get baptized!" Afterward, she learned that she had been present at adoration and benediction of the Blessed Sacrament when she heard the clear inner voice telling her that she must be baptized.

The Lord is there.

Another testimony comes from Brother Roger of Taizé, the ecumenical community of Catholics and Protestants. He himself belonged to the Reformed Church. In his diary, he writes about the little Romanesque Catholic church in the village and says that he likes to pray in it. Then he adds the following short sentence: "This place is inhabited."

What kind of presence is this presence of the Lord? Let me begin with a text from the Second Vatican Council, in its Constitution on the Sacred Liturgy, *Sacrosanctum Concilium*, which takes up the question: How is Christ present in the liturgy?

> To accomplish so great a work [of redemption], Christ is always present in His Church, especially in her liturgical celebrations. He is present in the sacrifice of the Mass, not only in the person of His minister, "the same now offering, through the ministry of priests, who formerly offered himself on the cross", but especially under the Eucharistic species. By His power He is present in the sacraments, so that when a man baptizes it is really Christ Himself who baptizes.

---

[1] *Das Buch meines Lebens* [The book of my life] (Graz, 1981).

He is present in His word, since it is He Himself who speaks when the holy scriptures are read in the Church. He is present, lastly, when the Church prays and sings, for He promised: "Where two or three are gathered together in my name, there am I in the midst of them."[2]

We need only add something that is not stated explicitly in the conciliar constitution but belongs to the core of the gospel: the Lord is present especially in those whom he calls "the least of my brothers". "I was naked and you clothed me, I was sick and you visited me, I was in prison and you came to me.... Truly, I say to you, as you did it to one of the least of these my brethren, you did it to me" (Mt 25:35–40). Christ's presence can also be experienced in the sacrament of my neighbor, especially when my neighbor needs my help.

The council declares that he is "especially" present in the eucharistic species, and that is the subject of the present catechesis. What does this word "especially" mean? Why do we seek in a special way the presence of Christ in the sacrament? At the end of this chapter, I will say something about eucharistic adoration.

Forms of Presence

Let us begin with a simple question: How is someone or something present? In an obvious, immediate sense we could say that when we come together somewhere, in Saint Stephen's Cathedral or at home, we are present, and we are present to one another. We are there. We can call this the simple *bodily,*

---

[2] *Sacrosanctum Concilium* 7. Quotations from the Council of Trent (session 22, *Doctrine on the Holy Sacrifice of the Mass*, chap. 2) and Mt 18:20.

physical presence. It is the precondition of our being there. If I get stuck in traffic on my way to hold a catechesis in our cathedral, then you would be there, but I would not be there. Or if one of the participants changed his mind and stayed at home because he was too tired, then he would not be there. The benches in Saint Stephen's and the furniture at home are also "there", but not in the same way as *we* are there. Furniture, walls, and pillars are there, but we mean something else when we say that *we* are "there". Presence means more than merely being located in one particular place. It implies being there for something or for someone.

We are talking, therefore, about being present in *relational* terms, being present with an attentive spirit. For example, when two people have a conversation, they are present for each other. It is, of course, also possible for people to be present exclusively in the physical sense of the term. When I board a train, I am undeniably present. The other travelers are present too, and one kind of relationship does come into existence between us, but it is neither intentional nor conscious. Sometimes, one falls into conversation with other travelers on a train. The individuals are no longer there just by themselves; a real relationship is established. Two, three, or more people talk with one another and are present for one another.

Mere physical presence is not enough: we need attentiveness as well, and this is directed toward someone in such a way that the bodily presence is accompanied by a *mental presence*. Philosophers call this "intentional presence", the orientation to another person. It is only the combination of bodily and mental presence that establishes the *personal presence* that is expressed most beautifully in friendship, where people are both *with* each other and *for* each other. This is a companionship of the soul, not a mere physical proximity;

and Saint Thomas calls friendship a *mutua inhaesio*, literally, a "reciprocal being in one another"—a marvelous phrase! This presence is living and intense. When Jesus speaks of his love for the Father, he says that they are "in" each other: "I in you and you in me" (Jn 17:21). This is the strongest form of presence; without it, a purely physical presence is colorless and lifeless. It can even be loveless. When two people love each other or are friends, they yearn to be with each other, and they value their mutual presence very highly.

Sometimes, of course, being together can be intolerable. The Bible is well aware of this. Let me quote a drastic aphorism from the Old Testament: "It is better to live in a corner of the housetop than in a house shared with a contentious woman" (Prov 21:9; 25:24). It was, of course, a man who wrote those words . . . but I imagine that a woman could have said something similar on her own account.

There are, however, situations in which there is no bodily presence. Friends do not see each other for a long period, and lovers are separated. But in their memory, in the intention of their wills, and in the devotion of their hearts they are close to each other. It is possible to remain vividly present to each other even when we see the other seldom or never, and live far apart. In such a situation, it is particularly important that we remain present to each other. Two lovers who are separated by external circumstances are nevertheless very close to each other in their thoughts and in their love, even without the physical presence. And this is a perfectly real presence; the only thing lacking is the physical dimension.

Many years ago, the media told the story of a Cuban writer who was imprisoned by Fidel Castro for twenty-two years. He was thrown into prison as a young man, shortly after his wedding day, and his wife waited twenty-two years— eight thousand days and nights—for him. Love of this kind entails a very strong form of presence, something that is profoundly real. And it makes the lack of physical presence all the more painful.

Let us attempt to grasp this point more deeply. The decisive aspect of personal presence is the spiritual presence of the mind or soul; we could call this the personal dimension of presence. This mental presence longs for physical presence. One wants to see one's friends again, and lovers who have been separated want to be reunited. Physical and spatial separation are experienced as a disturbance, but they cannot destroy this presence of the mind.

There is, however, a third form of presence, which we might call the *presence in the form of a sign*. I may not have the physical presence of the one whom I love, or of my friend, but I do possess a photograph. Fathers proudly show photographs of their children. These are signs and souvenirs that give life to the presence of the mind, and in one sense they can even sometimes take the place of bodily presence.

Leonardo Boff—whose theology I do not share in other respects—has written a very beautiful little book about the sacraments in which he recalls the time when he was studying in Germany and his sister wrote to tell him that their father was dying.[3] It was impossible for Boff to return home to Brazil, and a second letter told him that their father had died. His sister sent him the butt of a cigarette—the last cigarette that his father had smoked. This was a sign that moved Boff very deeply—but for anyone else who might happen to find this cigarette butt somewhere, it would mean nothing at all.

One person may cherish his grandfather's old hat reverently, whereas another person would see only a battered

[3] *Sacraments of Life: Life of the Sacraments*, trans. John Drury (Washington, D.C.: Pastoral Press, 1987).

old hat that is worthless and ought to be thrown out. For the grandfather's grandson, it may perhaps be an important sign. A sign of this kind can create a relationship or keep a relationship alive. A souvenir, a picture, a photograph—the sign makes someone present, although, of course, it does so only for one who can read the sign. Some years ago, my family was given a very old photograph album with pictures of old aunts and uncles. We had no idea who these ancestors were, but fortunately, a great-aunt of mine was still alive, one hundred years old, and she could identify the faces on many of the photographs. Suddenly, they took on a meaning that they would not otherwise have had.

This presence of a sign is alive only to the extent that we can identify the sign. When we know what it signifies, the sign becomes strong and creates a presence. Otherwise, it is completely meaningless. I take good care of a spoon that my father always had with him when he served as a soldier in wartime, and it is highly meaningful for me. It is a sign that makes him present. But for someone who is unaware of this connection, it has no special significance.

The veneration of relics reflects something of this appreciation of signs. A portion of the body or the clothing of a person who lived in a particularly close relationship with God the Father or with Jesus makes that person present for us. Relics bring us to the threshold where these three kinds of presence meet: the presence of the body, of the mind, and of the sign.

Eucharist: Real Presence of Christ

What about the Eucharist? Our starting point is our faith that Christ is truly present—and this applies to all three forms of presence. A sign is a genuine presence: not a bodily presence but a powerful presence of the mind. We have already seen that the presence of the mind is something powerful and real. In other words, the bodily presence is not the only real presence. What then does this mean for the genuine presence of Christ in the Eucharist, which the Church's teaching calls the *real* presence?

Let us begin by recalling that the presence of the mind longs for bodily presence. One who loves wishes to be physically present to the other. Christ, however, is no longer physically present among us. Is it possible to encounter him in the mind? Doubtless, this is possible in memory, in prayer, in love. And what about the presence in the form of a sign? This too is possible. Let us imagine someone entering a church where Mass is being celebrated. He sees the priest lift up a piece of bread while all fall silent; then the priest genuflects. One who does not understand the sign cannot enter into any relationship with what is going on.

One objection has often been made: Christ is in heaven, so how is it possible for him to be really present in the Eucharist? Surely he cannot be in heaven *and* bodily present among us at one and the same time? The Church's teaching replies that the sacraments are signs that are comprehensible only when one knows what they signify. Baptism employs water and words; confirmation employs an anointing and the laying on of hands; priestly ordination employs the laying on of hands; and the anointing of the sick employs oil.

In our preparation for First Holy Communion, we learned that bread and wine are signs—but what kind of signs? How can they bring Christ near to us? They are certainly not like photographs. We do not see the physical form of Christ, and the bread does not have the shape of his body. He is not physically present in the way that we are physically present in our homes. Nevertheless, it is clear that the bread was an important sign: in the Gospel story of the disciples on the road to Emmaus, we read that "he was known to them in the breaking of the bread" (Lk 24:35). Clearly, this sign meant a great deal to the disciples. When he broke the bread, this was something that reminded them of Jesus; and more than that, this was, in fact, how they recognized him. In the language of faith, we say that Christ is present under the form of bread. We believe that it has truly become his Body, although the form of bread remains unaltered.

Reflecting on signs can help us to understand how Jesus is present in the Eucharist. It is his gift to us, but it is not like a bouquet of flowers—although that too would be a sign. If I visit someone and bring flowers, that is certainly a sign. When a married couple quarrels, and the husband then brings flowers and gives them to his wife with a loving gesture, this bouquet functions as a very eloquent sign.

It is in the sign of bread that Jesus wishes to be specially present to us. What does this sign tell us? Bread is nourishment. When Jesus said, "Take and eat", and gave the disciples bread with the words "This is my body", he obviously wished to *show* something by means of this sign. He is so present to us in the bread that we can draw life from him. He is present to us as our food. Bread is a staple element in our diet, something essential to life, while wine is for feasts. Through these signs of bread and wine, Christ indicates that he wants to be present for us both in everyday life with its cares and in the joy of a feast.[4]

---

[4] See R. Messner, *Einführung in die Liturgiewissenschaft* [Introduction to liturgical theology] (Paderborn, 2001), p. 209.

When he breaks the bread for us and gives us the cup of wine, he tells us that he wishes to be physically and spiritually present to us in one particular way. He wants to be our food, and he wants to be present for us in friendship: "He who eats my flesh and drinks my blood abides in me, and I in him" (Jn 6:56).

He wants to be so close to us that he gives us himself as our nourishment. Here the sign is decisive, and this is why we never abandon this particular sign. The Church requires the use of bread in the Mass—not rice or polenta. Even in Africa and Asia, the Mass is celebrated with bread, not with manioc, for the simple reason that he chose *this* sign. He wishes to give himself to us with a sign that is tied to one particular history, to one particular place, and to one particular tradition, a sign that has one particular meaning. This is how he wishes to be received by us, and this is how he wishes to receive us.

"I love you so much that I could eat you up." This turn of phrase suggests that our language has retained at least something of the presence of this sign. We cannot, of course, apply these words directly to the eucharistic presence, but there is surely some faint echo here.

Signs are intended to communicate something. When I am driving and see a rectangular sign with the number 50, this is an unambiguous indication that one is not allowed to drive at 100 miles per hour. When Christ employs the sign of bread, he wishes to indicate that he is so completely present for us that he gives himself as our food.

Is this the presence only of a sign? Some have argued that the bread is only a sign that reminds us of Jesus, like my grandfather's hat or the photograph that stands on my table and reminds me of my grandmother. All the signs that we know point to something other than themselves. But this sign contains what it signifies. We could say that it points to itself. This sign of bread points to the one who said, "This is my body." And this makes it a wholly unique sign.

Only faith allows us to grasp what kind of presence this is. In this sign, the Lord unites both his bodily and his spiritual presence, although the word "bodily" does not refer here to the physical mass of his earthly body. The Church's teaching uses an important term here: the Lord is *essentially* present in this sign, not in his physical body but with his entire being, *vere, realiter, substantialiter*—truly present, really (i.e., effectively) present, and substantially present. It is he himself, with his Body and soul and his Godhead.[5]

In the last analysis, we stand before a sign. Those who cannot share our Catholic faith may perhaps find it a meaningful sign that helps us remember Jesus—"Do this in memory of me!"—but our faith says much more than this. Through the consecration, the Lord himself is present in this sign, genuinely, truly, and substantially.

The faith that recognizes this is not blind; rather, the sign leads it to the reality. "Take and eat! This is my body." The sign tells us what the Lord wants to do in our lives. Take, eat, receive me, my Body, my soul, my divinity, all of me. Take and drink, for this is my Blood, shed for you for the forgiveness of sins.

The Presence of the Lord and the Life of the Church

I conclude with three brief additional remarks connected with the Church's teaching.

[5] See *CCC* 1374.

First, how long does the presence in the Eucharist last? What I have written above makes the answer clear: the presence lasts as long as the sign is there. The presence of the Lord is tied to the sign. He gives himself to us under the forms of bread and wine. If it is no longer wine or no longer bread, then this presence of the Lord ceases to exist.[6] I can receive the Lord in Holy Communion. The sacramental presence lasts as long as I have the bread in me, that is, while I am eating it, and indeed until it is digested. Naturally, the presence of his grace remains beyond this time, and I can always turn to him in prayer, in intercession, in an act of love and devotion. The *sacramental* presence is tied to the form. We may therefore draw the practical conclusion that as long as the Communion is in us, we should not take up our daily activities, and this is why it is so meaningful and important to spend some time in silence, in adoration, and in thanksgiving after receiving Communion: Now I have received you in the sacrament, now I am with you as you are with me.

This is why I have asked for the observation of a period of silence after Communion in the Masses in our diocese, a time of intimacy with Christ, whom we have received in the sacrament. For the same reason, it is good (wherever possible) not to rush out of the church at the end of Mass to get on with one's daily activities. The Mass is a tremendous event, and we should pause to let it resonate within us.

Second, we have the "reserved" sacrament in the tabernacle. The sacramental presence is tied to the form, the sign of bread and wine, and this means that this presence continues to exist after the Mass. Normally, we drink all

---

[6] See *CCC* 1377.

the contents of the chalice, but we keep the Hosts in the
tabernacle for the sick. This practice goes back to the early
Church, where some of the sacrament was left over, so
that Communion could be brought to the sick; and Christians realized very early on that we cannot simply leave
the eucharistic bread in a drawer in the kitchen, as if it
were ordinary bread. It is the sacred Body of the Lord,
even after the Mass. This is why the remaining Hosts have
always been kept with particular care. Gradually, the adoration of the eucharistic species outside Mass began. The
Church holds that the tabernacle should have a special place
of honor and should be accessible even outside the times
of Mass, so that we can spend time before the eucharistic
Lord.[7]

> Adoro te devote, latens Deitas,
> quae sub his figuris vere latitas:
> tibi se cor meum totum subicit,
> quia te contemplans totum deficit
> (Thomas Aquinas)

In the translation by Gerard Manley Hopkins:

Godhead here in hiding, whom I do adore
masked by these bare shadows, shape and nothing more,
see, Lord, at thy service low lies here a heart
lost, all lost in wonder at the God thou art.

Third, this very simple form of eucharistic adoration is
very important! Many people are critical; after all, they point
out, Jesus told us, "Take and eat." He did not say, "Take
and look at me; adore the eucharistic species!" How then
is this adoration to be justified? This polemical argument

[7] See *CCC* 1379.

has been employed against eucharistic adoration again and again.

It is perfectly true that bread is meant to be eaten. But when we adore the Lord under the appearance of bread, he is present to us precisely in the form in which he wants to give himself to us, and eucharistic adoration reminds us of this: "See, I exist for you to such a degree that I am here for you to eat. I in you and you in me." [8] Adoration makes us aware of the depths of this mystery.

One of the most celebrated conversion stories of the twentieth century is that of the well-known French journalist André Frossard. Many people have read his book *I Have Met Him: God Exists*. His parents were atheists and brought him up without religious faith. He studied at the best-known elite university in France, the École normale supérieure in the rue d'Ulm in Paris, and was a brilliant young intellectual. One day, he wanted to visit a friend and heard that he had gone into the chapel of a convent on the other side of the street from his college. André Frossard too went into the chapel in search of his friend. He writes: "I went in. Ten minutes later, I came back out as a Christian." This was one of those overwhelming conversion experiences that occur from time to time. Looking back, André Frossard was able to unlock the mystery of his conversion. The sisters in the rue d'Ulm in Paris practiced perpetual adoration, and he subsequently understood that the one who had entered his life so suddenly was there, present in the Eucharist. It was he who had called Frossard.

I believe that the simplest expression of the mystery was formulated by the parish priest of Ars: "*Il est là*. He is there."

---

[8] See *CCC* 1379–80.

8

"HE WHO EATS THIS BREAD ..."— COMMUNION

We now come to the final part of the Mass, to Holy Communion. Those who go to Mass regularly are familiar with the words that are spoken before Communion: "Lord, I am not worthy that you should enter under my roof, but only say the word and my soul shall be healed." These words are taken from the Gospel. A Roman centurion in Capernaum comes to Jesus and asks him to heal his servant. But since he is a Gentile, a Roman, and knows that a believing Jew is not permitted to enter the house of an unbeliever, he says these moving words: "Lord, I am not worthy to have you come under my roof; but only say the word, and my servant will be healed" (Mt 8:8). This prayer has been said before Communion for many centuries. We identify with the Roman centurion and confess that we are unworthy to have the Lord enter us, our house, our life.

I wish to hold a catechesis, not an academic lecture, about Holy Communion. Naturally, a catechesis too includes doctrine, but the word "catechesis" itself literally means an "echo from above", an echo of the doctrine, in amazement at what we hear and what we do, in response to the greatness of what happens in the Eucharist. In addition to being the Church's teaching, our catechesis will be a reflection, perhaps an astounding reflection, on the greatness of what happens in Holy Communion. We need to reflect more frequently and deeply on these realities.

> O sacrum convivium, in quo Christus sumitur; recolitur memoria passionis eius, mens impletur gratia et futurae gloriae nobis pignus datur, alleluia.

> O sacred banquet in which Christ is received as food, the memory of his passion is renewed, the soul is filled with grace, and a pledge of the glory to come is given to us, alleluia.[1]

Three chapters are devoted to Holy Communion. First of all, I follow the sequence of the liturgy: preparation for Communion, the reception of the sacrament, and the period after Communion. What is the fruit of Holy Communion when we receive it aright? The next two chapters take up a number of difficult and disputed questions about the reception of Holy Communion. Who is allowed to receive Communion, and who is not allowed, and under what circumstances? Three questions are particularly difficult, and we must not evade them when we speak about Communion.

It may perhaps be rare for the *first* question to be put explicitly: What are my personal dispositions? What does it mean to say "Lord, I am not worthy" each time we are about to receive the sacrament? Is this merely an empty formula, a cliché, or do we take it seriously? What does this mean for my reception of the sacrament? Are there situations in which I should refrain from receiving it?

The *second* difficult topic that is often raised is like a wound that keeps on breaking open: May those who are divorced and remarried receive the sacrament? There are numerous such people today, and their situation in the Church is

---

[1] *Magnificat* antiphon at Evening Prayer on the feast of Corpus Christi; see *CCC* 1402.

extremely difficult and painful, especially with regard to the
reception of the sacraments. The following chapter, on the
boundaries of the reception of Holy Communion, examines this question.

The *third* question too is much disputed: What about
eucharistic fellowship beyond the visible boundaries of the
various Christian confessions, so-called intercommunion
between Catholics and Protestants, or the sharing in the
sacrament with the other Christian churches and confessions? I will discuss this in the brief final chapter of this
book.

At the very outset, therefore, we can see that Holy Communion involves difficult and controversial questions.

The Indispensable Preparation

Let us begin with the preparation. We prepare ourselves for
all the important moments in life. It may, of course, happen that we are thrown unprepared into an important and
decisive situation, but when we are aware that something
big is about to happen, we prepare for the event. This preparation takes place in two phases. The *immediate preparation*
can sometimes be hectic—especially if it is not accompanied by a *long-term preparation*.

Let me take a very simple example. We are expecting an
important guest. The immediate preparation is clear: the
house is tidied up, and we try to ensure that everything the
guest may happen to see is neat and clean. Anything that is
untidy is hidden where he will hopefully not see it. We put
on our best clothes; we collect our thoughts and ponder,
"What will I say? What will we talk about?" There is thus
both an inner and an outer preparation.

In such moments, however, we also see whether there is a long-term preparation. This concerns lifestyle, basic attitudes, education, and the work I do on my own person, and it can take years or even decades. It is part of the preparation for an important moment in my life, and it comes into play when that moment arrives.

The preparation can be oriented to one specific goal or be more general. Education is a general preparation for life; and the work I do on my own person is preparation in a broader sense. There is also the preparation where all our energies are directed to one event; if things are to go well, we must bear in mind every aspect and make a thorough preparation.

What about our preparation for Holy Communion? The way in which we prepare reveals what Communion means to us. When we reflect on who it is that we receive in the sacrament, who it is that comes to us, we will feel a great desire to prepare ourselves. Experience shows, however, that routine and custom take the fine edge off this preparation, so that we tend to neglect it.

If I continually endeavor over the years to prepare myself for the sacrament, this establishes a basic inner attitude, an orientation to this event, which will accompany me always. If I know that I will receive Holy Communion next Sunday (or perhaps even tomorrow), this resonates consciously or unconsciously in all that I do today, and the entire day is marked either by the awareness that I will soon receive the sacrament or by the echo in me of the sacrament that I have received.

Help in Making One's Preparation

A number of things can help us to prepare more consciously for the great moment of Communion. One of these is no longer so vividly present in the consciousness of Catholic Christians, namely, fasting. The older generation still remembers that we had to fast from midnight before receiving the sacrament. A child who forgot this and ate a sweet without thinking could not receive Communion on Sunday morning. This precept was lightened first by Pope Pius XII (died 1958) and then in the course of the liturgical reforms after the Second Vatican Council, with the best of intentions. Initially, the fast was reduced to three hours before Communion, and then to one hour. Canon 919 §1 of the 1983 Code of Canon Law formulates the precept as follows: "A person who is to receive the Most Holy Eucharist is to abstain for at least one hour before Holy Communion from any food and drink, except for only water and medicine." Naturally, such a precept is not absolutely necessary. The decisive question is not whether or not I have eaten; Christ has set us free, and we are not dependent on dietary regulations. But this precept helps us to remember what we are doing.

Many people have a "memory function" in their mobile phones—at the appropriate time, the telephone rings to remind them of what they must do. Similarly, the law about fasting helps us to remember that we should prepare for Communion; we should not receive the sacrament without reflecting on what we are doing. I myself find one hour too little, for that is exactly the time it takes to get to church. There is therefore no problem about not eating food and drinking only water in the hour immediately before one receives Communion. Canon law says "except for only water and medicine". Perhaps this precept offers us a simple support that we have neglected. We are human beings of body and soul. If the soul is to be alert, it needs bodily signs that help it.

Let me add a practical observation. We cannot claim that abstinence from meat on Fridays is absolutely necessary; and in the past, there was often a measure of hypocrisy here, when people ate an expensive fish on Fridays instead of meat that was not so dear. But the fact that all Catholics were reminded by this precept that they should not eat meat helped them at the very least to remember that Friday was a special day on which we recall the death of Jesus that brought us redemption. Christ has set us free from such rules, true enough, and they are not necessary for salvation. But they are a help!

The Immediate Preparation in the Mass

How do we prepare in the Sunday Mass for Communion? What kind of immediate preparation takes place? The event itself surpasses our understanding. We believe that it is truly Christ who comes to us in Communion, and the entire celebration of the Mass is one great preparation for this encounter.

The preparation begins with the common confession of our sins. We then listen to the directives that Jesus gives for our life. We recall the mighty deeds of God for his people in history, culminating in the sending of Jesus, his death, and his Resurrection. All this becomes a present reality when the Mass is celebrated: "Take and eat; this is my body!" The great mystery of faith, the consecration, prepares us to take and eat. For example, we pray in the third canon: "Grant that we, who are nourished by the Body and Blood of your Son and filled with his Holy Spirit, may become one body, one spirit in Christ." We pray that the Holy Spirit may help us to receive Communion aright, so that it can bear fruit in us. The formulation in the second canon is simple and direct: "Humbly we pray that, partaking of the Body and Blood of Christ, we may be gathered into one by the Holy Spirit." The language in the third prayer after the consecration in the so-called Roman Canon, the first eucharistic prayer, is particularly impressive, with its very ancient—I might almost say "archaic"—character.

> In humble prayer we ask you, almighty God: command that these gifts be borne by the hands of your holy Angel to your altar on high in the sight of your divine majesty, so that all of us, who through this participation at the altar receive the most holy Body and Blood of your Son, may be filled with every grace and heavenly blessing.

The immediate preparation for Holy Communion begins with the *Lord's Prayer*. The unanimous tradition of the Church has always seen the request for bread as referring also to Communion: "Give us this day our daily bread" is thus also a request for the Body of the Lord. This prayer also reminds us that the preparation for the sacrament also entails a request for forgiveness of our guilt: "Forgive us our trespasses as we forgive those who trespass against us." Willingness to forgive others is a precondition for the right reception of Holy Communion.

Saint Augustine explains with infectious enthusiasm why the Lord's Prayer is spoken before we receive the Lord's Body:

> Why is it spoken before the reception of Christ's Body and Blood? For the following reason: If perchance, in conse-quence of human frailty, our thought seized on something indecent, if our tongue spoke something unjust, if our eye was turned to something unseemly, if our ear listened com-placently to something unnecessary . . . it is blotted out by

the Lord's Prayer in the passage: Forgive us our debts, so that we may approach in peace and so that we my not eat or drink what we receive unto judgment.[2]

In another sermon, Augustine compares the Lord's Prayer, which is the immediate preparation for Communion, with washing one's face. Before going forward to the altar, we cleanse ourselves, so that we may come to Christ with newly washed faces.[3]

The other prayers with which we are so familiar also help prepare us for the sacrament. After the Lord's Prayer, the priest prays, "Deliver us, Lord, we pray, from every evil, . . . [that] we may be always free from sin and safe from all distress, as we await the blessed hope and the coming of our Savior, Jesus Christ." This refers to the Lord's future coming in glory, but we can also understand it as a reference to his coming in the hour of our death—and to his coming now in the Eucharist.

In the prayer before the *sign of peace*, we ask, "Look not on our sins, but on the faith of your Church." This too is a preparation for Communion. This applies in a special way to the sign of peace, which the deacon invites us to exchange: "Let us offer each other the sign of peace." In April 2004, the Holy See issued an instruction on the liturgy, *Redemptionis Sacramentum*. I believe that this document is right to state that one should exchange the sign of peace in such a way that chaos is avoided in the church.[4] It is enough to give our neighbor the sign of peace—we need not run hither and thither, grabbing as many hands as possible.

---

[2] *Sermon Denis 6*; translation in Joseph A. Jungmann, *The Mass of the Roman Rite* (London: Burns and Oates, 1959), p. 465.

[3] See *Sermon 17*, 5,5; Patrologia latina 38:127.

[4] *Redemptionis Sacramentum* 72.

The *Agnus Dei* follows, during the breaking of the bread and the placing of a small piece of the Host in the chalice. Those who know the great tradition of classical music are familiar with the marvelous settings of these words by the Viennese composers. Their music is a perfect accompaniment to the intimate preparation for the reception of Christ's Body.

Then the door to the mystery is opened: "Behold the Lamb of God, behold him who takes away the sins of the world. Blessed are those called to the supper of the Lamb." The people respond to these words of the priest with the declaration of the Roman centurion: "Lord, I am not worthy that you should enter under my roof, but only say the word and my soul shall be healed."

The liturgical texts of the Christian East are often much more florid and detailed than our own, and it is interesting to see how these words have been elaborated there. One particularly vivid and moving prayer in preparation for Holy Communion runs as follows:

> Lord, I am not worthy that you should enter under the stained roof of my soul, but as you accepted to be laid down in a cave and a manger for dumb animals, and to enter the house of Simon the leper, and to receive, when she approached you, the sinful woman who resembled me: deign to enter both into the manger of my senseless soul and into my rubbish-filled body [which is that] of a dead and leprous [man]. And as you did not recoil when the filthy mouth of the sinful woman kissed your spotless feet, likewise, my Master and God, do not shun the sinner that I am, but in your goodness and love for mankind grant that I may become a communicant of your all-holy body and blood.[5]

---

[5] Translation: Joseph Raya and José de Vinck, *Byzantine Daily Worship* (Allendale, N.J.: Alleluia Press, 1969), p. 292.

In the Byzantine Orthodox churches, everyone knows by heart the marvelous prayer: "O Son of God, bring me into communion today with your mystical supper. I shall not tell your enemies the secret, nor kiss you with Judas' kiss. But like the good thief I cry, 'Jesus, remember me when you come into your kingdom.'"[6]

Receiving Communion

Only faith can tell us what happens in Holy Communion; we cannot understand this with our reason. But we can assent to it with our heart.

Let me begin with an episode from the life of Saint Catherine of Siena. Blessed Raymond of Capua (died 1399), her confessor, who later became the master general of the Dominican Order, knew her very well and wrote a very accurate account of her life. He relates the following story. Once, while Catherine was preparing to receive Communion, the priest lifted up the Host with the words, "This is the Lamb of God . . .", and Catherine replied, "Lord, I am not worthy that you should enter under my roof. But say only one word and my soul will be healed." Suddenly, she heard an inner voice. Jesus said to her, "But I am worthy that you should enter into me." In other words: You are unworthy that I should enter into you, but I am worthy that you should enter into me. Raymond of Capua adds, "As soon as she had received Communion, it seemed to her as if her soul entered into the Lord and the Lord into her, as the fish enters the water and the water

---

[6] *CCC* 1386.

surrounds it completely. And she felt herself wholly absorbed in God." [7]

The saints' lives show us that Communion brings about an interior and profound union with Christ that encompasses the whole of one's existence. But how can we—ordinary believers—live Communion aright? This question has preoccupied the Church and her members down through the ages, and there has been a striking oscillation between two poles. Sometimes the one pole dominates, and sometimes the other.

On the one hand, there is the simple, almost childlike joy that the Lord Jesus is present for us so directly under the appearances of bread and wine. This leads to the deep desire to receive Communion frequently: "Give us today our daily bread." It is probable that people in the early Church received the sacrament often; the Church Fathers have many encouraging words about the praxis of daily Communion, since we need this as urgently as we need our daily bread. This trend obviously entails the risk that what is daily becomes humdrum. Reverence vanishes, superficiality ensues, and routine gets the upper hand.

This is why a contrary tendency has always coexisted: ponder what you are doing; reflect on who it is that is coming to you! Are you really prepared for this? The apostle Paul felt obliged to warn his beloved (and difficult) community in Corinth, those newly converted pagans, not to confuse Communion, the Body of the Lord, with an ordinary meal. He makes a very serious appeal to their consciences: "As often as you eat this bread and drink the chalice, you proclaim the Lord's death until he comes" (1 Cor 11:26). He then continues, using very clear language:

---

[7] *Legenda major* 2.4, 192.

Whoever, therefore, eats the bread or drinks the cup of the Lord in an unworthy manner will be guilty of profaning the body and blood of the Lord. Let a man examine himself, and so eat of the bread and drink of the cup. For any one who eats and drinks without discerning the body eats and drinks judgment upon himself. (11:27–29)

With reference to the concrete situation in his beloved Corinthian community, Paul goes on:

That is why many of you are weak and ill, and some have died. But if we judged ourselves truly, we should not be judged. But when we are judged by the Lord, we are chastened so that we may not be condemned along with the world. So then, my brethren, when you come together to eat, wait for one another. (11:30–33)

He has already complained that some have too much to eat and are indeed already drunk, while the others go hungry. Now he writes, "If any one is hungry, let him eat at home— lest you come together to be condemned. About the other things I will give directions when I come" (11:34) Examine yourselves, judge yourselves, and then you will not be judged! Unfortunately, we do not know what Paul said on his next visit to Corinth. In this passage, he recalls the seriousness of the Lord's Supper. It must not be confused with ordinary food!

On the one hand, we ought to receive Communion frequently. It is good to do so every time we take part in the Mass, if at all possible: "Take and eat!" On the other hand, we ought to live in such a way that it *is* indeed possible for us to receive the Body of the Lord every day. The question of frequency is thus closely linked to the question of the quality of my life. Am I well prepared? Is my life in harmony with Holy Communion? Is the reception of the sacrament something that accords with the rest of my life?

There is, of course, a justified objection that can be made at this point: Is not Holy Communion a medicine? Did not Jesus say, "Those who are well have no need of a physician, but those who are sick" (Mt 9:12 and parallels)? Is it not precisely we sinners who need the Body of the Lord? Obviously, all of this is true. But we need him to *heal* us—and this presupposes that we first recognize and confess our sins, so that we may approach the Lord in the right way. If we do not show the physician our wounds, he cannot heal them.

As far as the reception of Holy Communion is concerned, there is much that is positive today, but there are also difficulties. I remember my time as a young priest in the Wienviertel district of Lower Austria. In those days, older people never received Communion without first going to confession, and this meant that Communion was a rare event. This was a remnant of the praxis that had been changed at the beginning of the twentieth century by Pope Saint Pius X (died 1914), who wanted the doors to Holy Communion to be opened as early and as wide as possible. This position was reinforced and deepened by the Second Vatican Council.

The danger we encounter today is banality. Receiving Communion has become so much a matter of course that we are entitled to ask: Do we "discern" the Body of the Lord? Are we sufficiently prepared? I celebrate many Masses at which almost everyone in the church comes forward to receive Holy Communion, and I often ask myself: Are we really prepared? (I include myself in this question!) On the one hand, therefore, I am glad that so many come; on the other, I fear that this may have become an automatic action. How alive is our faith in the true Body of Christ that we receive?

Some people believe that Communion in the hand is to blame; it is alleged that this praxis has dealt reverence a deadly blow. I myself believe that Communion can be received with great reverence in the hand. When I distribute Holy Communion, I see perfectly well whether people are receiving Communion in the hand reverently. Besides this, I believe that more sins are committed with the tongue than with the hand. The tongue is an instrument that does very evil things. If the Lord does not disdain to come onto my sinful tongue, then he will certainly not disdain to come into my hand! This is a question of my inner attitude, a question of reverence.

I am always impressed when I see how Orthodox Christians receive Communion. The sacrament is always administered under both kinds. The priest dips the Body of Christ into his Blood and places it on the tongue of the communicants. I recall here my Russian friends, whom I often visited in their home in Switzerland. When this family, or even just one child of the family, received Holy Communion, it was a great event. They made ready and put on their finest clothes. Naturally, they went to confession in the Orthodox manner. It was a great feast day. After the liturgy, they had a special meal at home to mark the fact that one child, or the entire family, had received Christ.

Are we fully aware of what it means to have received the Body of the Lord on Sunday? The reverent attitude—irrespective of whether we receive Holy Communion on the tongue or in the hand—is an expression of our faith.

What then are we to do? Christ himself has given us some important pointers. Let me mention only two passages in the Gospel that are relevant here. "If you are offering your gift at the altar, and there remember that your brother has something against you, leave your gift there before the altar and go; first be reconciled to your brother, and then come and offer your gift" (Mt 5:23–24). Am I really going to receive Communion when my heart refuses reconciliation, in a situation of bitter strife or even hatred? If I hesitate to receive the sacrament, I am reacting in the spirit of the Gospel.

We find a second pointer in the parable of the royal wedding feast, which recalls Communion, the marriage feast of the Lamb. We hear of a man who has no wedding garment. When the king asks him, "Friend, how did you get in here without a wedding garment?" the man does not reply. What happens next is not what we would expect: "Then the king said to the attendants, 'Bind him hand and foot, and cast him into the outer darkness'" (Mt 22:11–13). This is a warning. Jesus is asking, "How well are you prepared?"

This might, of course, lead us to say in fear, "But I am never prepared . . ." That would not be the right response. The words "Lord, I am not worthy" will always be true. But the preparation for the sacrament consists simply and precisely in recalling who it is that is coming to me, and then turning to him, asking for his help, and rejoicing in his mercy. This is the preparation that is required before he can enter under the roof of my poor hut.

9

BOUNDARIES OF THE RECEPTION OF COMMUNION

The last two chapters of this book take up the painful question of the boundaries of eucharistic fellowship. This concerns the fellowship that Christians have with one another, the ecumenical question of unity or disunity in the Lord's Supper. But it also concerns the situation inside the Catholic Church, for example, the question whether or not those who have divorced and remarried may be admitted to the sacraments. This painful question is asked often today.

If Jesus himself came for everyone, why is the concrete realization of this gift in the Eucharist not open to everyone? If Christ's love is boundless, why does the eucharistic fellowship have boundaries? If Christ died and rose for everyone, why does not everyone receive a share in the fruit of his death, that is, the Eucharist?

Eucharist and Baptism

The love of Christ knows no boundaries, and no one is excluded from this love. There are boundaries, however, around Communion. One absolutely indispensable boundary is the fact that the Lord's Supper, the Eucharist, is for those who are baptized.

Sometimes during Mass here in Saint Stephen's Cathedral or elsewhere, I see tourists coming forward to the Communion rails. They obviously do not know exactly what is going on, and I simply ask them, "Are you baptized?" If the answer is no, I shake hands with them or make a small gesture of blessing and wish them God's blessing. It is not a lack of love that makes me withhold Communion from them. Holy Communion is the meal of those who have become Jesus' disciples by means of baptism.

This does not mean that Jesus lived and died only for the baptized. He gave the apostles the commission "Go therefore and make disciples of all nations, baptizing them in the name of the Father and of the Son and of the Holy Spirit" (Mt 28:19).

Love knows no boundaries. Last week, a bishop from Burkina Faso in Africa visited me. He collaborates with the German Christoffel Mission to the Blind [Christoffel Blindenmission] and does outstanding work. Naturally, they do not ask for a baptismal certificate when a blind or partially sighted person comes to them! Everyone is welcome. They want to help everyone in need, for love knows no boundaries.

But the Supper of the Lord is the Supper for the baptized. The eucharistic fellowship with Christ is reserved to the baptized.

The only door for non-Christians to this eucharistic fellowship with Christ and the Church is the door of baptism. This has been clear since the very first day of the Church's history, at Pentecost in Jerusalem.

The fact that the Lord's Supper is reserved to the baptized also means that eucharistic fellowship presupposes fellowship in the faith. The Eucharist is the expression and the high point of fellowship in the faith. It is the table fellowship of Jesus' family, the family that is founded through faith and baptism. Eucharistic fellowship is the very heart, the innermost dimension, of this life in the fellowship of the family of Jesus.

Since the Eucharist is the goal and high point of life in this fellowship, it has entailed an intensive preparation from the earliest times onward. In the ancient Church, the preparation for baptism was a lengthy path that covered at least the period of Lent, and this is still the rule for all adults who receive baptism. It is only at the end of this path that one can be initiated into the innermost mysteries of the Christian faith and life. During the Easter Vigil the newly baptized are made members of the Church and are allowed to share in the Eucharist for the first time.

But if Communion is truly an encounter with the mercy of Jesus—I am not worthy, but he makes me worthy—why then do boundaries exist? Why are some persons excluded from Communion? Is not this clearly opposed to what Jesus himself did?

It is undeniably true that the love of God is without boundaries. But *I* can set limits to the love of God if I refuse to accept it. The love of Christ is without boundaries. But Holy Communion does have boundaries.

Necessary Boundaries

Let me first make two preliminary remarks. First, it is important to remember that boundaries are not per se a bad thing. Our bodies have boundaries. If they had no boundaries, they would not be bodies! Every form necessarily includes boundaries.

The fence in my garden separates it from my neighbor's garden, but it also joins them together. A boundary is always a *connecting* line too. We have our national boundaries, which tell us which territory is our native land. The town or city where we live has boundaries, and a family has boundaries—some boundaries are inside, and others are outside. It is only when we consciously accept these boundaries that they can also become connecting lines.

Boundaries are not a priori bad, and we should not be too quick to assume that they exist solely in order to keep people out.

Second, boundaries can be drawn from the inside or from the outside. I can fence myself in—or others can erect a fence with regard to me. Both are necessary. I need to establish boundaries, because otherwise there will be no structure in my life, my activities, and my relationships; and others too must establish their own boundaries if life in society is to succeed.

Let us apply these principles to the question of Holy Communion and eucharistic boundaries. There are boundaries with regard to eucharistic fellowship that I myself establish, and there are other boundaries that the community lays down for me. I can be open to this fellowship, but I can also withdraw from it and shut the door, for example, if I leave the fellowship of the Church. Through my own decision, I am no longer inside the boundaries of the fellowship of faith and communion. But it is also possible for the community to lay down boundaries in my regard, for example, if it is judged that my behavior is not in accordance with the rules of the community. This is a principle found wherever people come together as a body. It is not something specific to the Church.

Boundaries of the Eucharistic Community

How are boundaries drawn in the eucharistic community? In one instance, the apostle Paul draws a clear and unambiguous boundary. Incest has occurred in Corinth, and Paul takes the decisive step of excommunicating the person responsible. He excludes him from the community, but he explicitly states that the purpose is not to destroy him but to save him. Paul hopes that this man will come to his senses and abandon behavior that is damaging both himself and the community. When Paul thus excludes a person from the Corinthian community, he also excludes him from fellowship in the Lord's Supper (1 Cor 5:1ff.; 11:29).

There is, however, another way of dealing with potential boundaries, and Paul speaks of this too, when he reminds the Corinthians:

> Whoever, therefore, eats the bread or drinks the cup of the Lord in an unworthy manner will be guilty of profaning the body and blood of the Lord. Let a man examine himself, and so eat of the bread and drink of the cup. For any one who eats and drinks without discerning the body eats and drinks judgment upon himself. (1 Cor 11:27–29)

One must examine oneself and perhaps draw a boundary for oneself. See whether you are in fact "discerning" the Body of the Lord! There is a little play on words in the Greek text between *krina*, "judgment", and *diakrinon*, "discerning". If you do not discern that the Body of the Lord is different from ordinary bread, you are, so to speak, eating judgment upon yourself. This holy food brings judgment! Look carefully at your life, therefore. Perhaps you need to draw a boundary somewhere. Or perhaps you need to overcome a barrier that exists in your life before you can approach

the Body and Blood of the Lord, the bread and the chalice
of the Lord.

This is why a very ancient tradition of the Church pre-
scribes that one who is conscious of having committed a
grave sin and whose conscience is burdened may enter the
eucharistic fellowship only through the gate of the sacrament of penance.[1] This barrier must be overcome before
one can be restored to the community of those who receive
Holy Communion. Christ bestowed the authority to forgive sins in order that this fellowship might be reestab-
lished. Those who have excluded themselves from the family
of Jesus through wrong conduct can be reintegrated into
the Church through the forgiveness of their sins.

Sometimes, of course, a person does not realize that his
conduct has taken him over a boundary. It is then the task
of the pastors to draw the boundary, so that repentance is
possible.

This happened again and again in the life of Saint Pio of
Pietrelcina, "Padre Pio" (died 1968). During Mass, he would
suddenly turn around and look for one particular person in
the congregation. He would then point to him and say,
"*Via, via!* Get out of here, get out of here!" This was highly
unpleasant for the person concerned. A priest I know told
me about one such case, where a man was sent out of the
church by Padre Pio. It took the man three days to make
up his mind to go to confession, but the clear boundaries
that the priest had drawn were the salvation of this man.

There is a celebrated story from early Church history of
a drawing of boundaries. The exact details of this excommunication may perhaps be legendary, but it remains very
impressive. Emperor Theodosius the Great (died 395), who

[1] See *CCC* 1385.

did so much for the Christianization of the Roman Empire, crushed a rebellion with tremendous violence and had his troops slaughter seven thousand people in the stadium at Thessalonica. The emperor resided in Milan, and when he wished to enter the church in that city, Saint Ambrose, the bishop of Milan, refused him admittance and demanded that he do public penance for this crime of which he was guilty. Tradition relates that the emperor did penance and finally, after a lengthy penitential period, went barefoot into the church and threw himself to the ground as a sign of his repentance. Ambrose then reconciled him to the Church and lifted the excommunication.[2]

In this context, we must consider an important argument. The emperor was responsible for the massacre of seven thousand people, but when he did penance, he was readmitted to Communion. No matter how long the divorced and remarried may live, however, they are never readmitted. It is possible that the first marriage may be annulled (i.e., declared invalid), but when is it realistic—and honest—to expect this?

Many people have experienced the breakdown of their first sacramental marriage, which had been solemnly blessed in church, and have then entered a new relationship, a second marriage. Perhaps they are sincerely endeavoring to live a better Christian life in this second marriage than in the first; but they remain excluded from Communion (and the reception of the sacraments in general) for the rest of their lives. Is not the Church too hard, too obstinate, here? Why does she insist in this way on the indissolubility of marriage?

---

[2] *Patrologia latina* 16:1160–64; Hugo Rahner, *Kirche und Staat im frühen Christentum: Dokumente aus acht Jahrhunderten und ihre Deutung* (Munich, 1961), pp. 184–93 and 111–13.

Every pastor of souls knows how painful such situations can be—and so often are.

The rules of the Church are frequently criticized: "Why are they so harsh?" And many proposals have been made. For example, we ought to introduce a period of penance and then give ecclesial recognition in some form to the new relationship. Comparisons are drawn with the Eastern Church, which has a similar praxis. Why should not we do the same in the Catholic Church?

We can take this argument one step further. A murderer can go to confession and then receive the sacraments anew, but those who are divorced and remarried cannot do so. Does this make sense?

Naturally, things are not quite so simple. A priest cannot give absolution to a murderer unless the perpetrator is willing to accept the consequences of what he has done. He must surrender to the police and accept the penalty that the court will impose on him for his crime. If he is not willing to accept the penalty for his deed, he cannot receive absolution. This means that the comparison in the last paragraph is not perfect. Every absolution in the sacrament of confession presupposes that atonement will be made, as far as is possible, for the sins that have been committed.

Communion and the Christian Life

The difficult question of the admission of divorced and remarried persons to Holy Communion opens our eyes to a larger context. How do we deal with the boundaries to eucharistic fellowship that may have come into being in our own lives? How can we prepare ourselves with greater care to receive the sacrament? What ought I to do if I discover that I am insufficiently prepared? To take only one example: Can an employer who exploits his workers and treats them badly judge himself sufficiently prepared to receive Christ in Communion?

Have we perhaps forgotten the value of *spiritual communion*? Saint Teresa of Avila (died 1582) writes, "When you do not receive Communion ... but hear Mass, you can make a spiritual communion. Spiritual communion is highly beneficial; ... for the love of the Lord is thereby deeply impressed on the soul." [3] Spiritual communion can sometimes be valuable for all who make their preparation and discover that they are not wholly in accord with the sacrament they want to receive.

"Mom, today I'm going to Communion for you." This is a wonderful idea, showing an awareness of *communio*, in the sense of the fellowship that is the Church. For the Eucharist and Holy Communion are not only my personal encounter with my Jesus. The word *communio* always designates both the sacrament of the altar and the fellowship of the Church. It could often be helpful for us, when we receive Communion, to say, "Today I am going to Communion for this person or that, for those who cannot go or do not want to go, for those who are far off and have not yet found the path that leads to Christ." This is the Church's fellowship, this living community that knows that we are one body in Christ and that each of us is a member of this one body. One who for some reason is unable to receive sacramental Communion is not thereby excluded from this living fellowship of the body of Christ, and it is important that we

---

[3] Saint Teresa of Avila, *Way of Perfection* in *The Collected Works of Saint Teresa of Avila*, vol. 2, ed. Kieran Kavanaugh, O.C.D. and Otilio Rodriguez, O.C.D. (Washington, D.C.: ICS Publications, 1980), p. 174.

show these persons that they belong to the living fellowship of the body of Christ.

One final point: the fact that there are many persons in our parishes who sincerely endeavor to lead a Christian life but cannot receive Communion reminds us that we cannot take it as a matter of course that we are permitted to receive Christ in this way. We have no "claims" to grace. It is always a *gift* when we are permitted to go to the sacraments.

10

THE EUCHARIST AND ECUMENISM

If the Eucharist is the table fellowship of the baptized, why is it not open to all the baptized alike? It is precisely *this* question that makes us painfully aware of the wound that is Christian disunity: we are united by baptism and divided at the table of the Lord.

> That they may all be one; even as you, Father, are in me, and I in you, that they also may be in us, so that the world may believe that you have sent me. (Jn 17:21)

We have no "right" to grace. This was a fundamental idea of the Reformation, of Martin Luther and John Calvin, and our Protestant brothers and sisters today often point out that it is not we who invite to the Lord's Supper but Jesus himself. It is he who is the host; and since he is the one who extends the invitation, they believe that we cannot exclude anyone. They ask us: Why do not you Catholics—and above all, the bishops and the magisterium—accept this invitation and celebrate the Lord's Supper with us? Why is it so hard for you to come together with us to the Lord's Supper and to sit together at the table of the Lord?

One could discuss this question at great length, but I limit myself to offering a brief summary of the Church's teaching, followed by a simple recommendation for our praxis.

The Eucharist in the Christian Churches

To begin with, we make a distinction between those Churches where we believe that fully valid sacraments are celebrated, and those churches and ecclesial communities in which we believe that the whole fullness that is found in the Catholic Church is lacking.

We believe that the sacraments of the *Eastern churches* are valid. These churches possess not only valid baptism but also the valid Eucharist and the ordination of deacons, priests, and bishops, just as in the Catholic Church. In principle, eucharistic fellowship between Orthodox and Catholics is possible. All that is missing is the external ecclesiastical fellowship; and from the perspective of the sacrament, there is nothing that would essentially contradict such a fellowship.

This is why we say that one who is in an Orthodox country such as Russia, where there is no possibility of taking part in Catholic worship anywhere near at hand, can receive the sacraments there, provided that the Orthodox themselves allow this. This is our position; the Orthodox see things differently, and most of them do not in fact allow us to receive the sacraments in their churches.

The situation of the *churches and ecclesial communities born of the Reformation* is different, because they lack the sacrament of ordination of priests and bishops. This is why we believe that they lack the fullness of the Eucharist as this is celebrated in the Orthodox and the Catholic churches. This does not mean that the Protestant Lord's Supper is simply "nothing". Let me quote the words of the Second Vatican Council here: "When they commemorate [the Lord's] death and resurrection in the Lord's Supper, they profess that it signifies life in communion with Christ and look forward to His coming in glory."[1] The Protestant Lord's Supper is thus certainly fellowship with Christ but not in the way that we Catholics understand the Eucharist.

Communion for Non-Catholics?

There are numerous situations where Protestant and Catholic Christians live together, for example, in mixed marriages. What are we to say about the question of *intercommunion*? Can a Christian from another confession receive Holy Communion in the Catholic Mass?

All that we do in our relationships between the confessions ought to be marked by truthfulness. It must be done in love but also in truth. Despite all that we have in common, we should not merely gloss over the differences.

I have a very simple rule. It is not my own invention, but I find it convincing. I tell our Protestant brothers and sisters: One who says "Amen" to the Body of Christ in Holy Communion must also be able to say the "Amen" at the end of the eucharistic prayer, even as a non-Catholic Christian. In the eucharistic prayer, a transformation takes place: bread and wine are consecrated and become the Body and Blood of Christ. The Communion cannot be separated from the eucharistic prayer in the totality of its form.

One who can say the "Amen" to the eucharistic prayer can also say the "Amen" to Communion. This is at the very least a personal rule that offers a guideline.

Let us take the third eucharistic prayer, wherein the priest prays:

[1] *Unitatis Redintegratio* 22; see also *CCC* 1400.

Look, we pray, upon the oblation of your Church and, recognizing the sacrificial Victim by whose death you willed
to reconcile us to yourself . . .

We believe that the Mass is *this holy and living sacrifice*, the
sacrifice of Christ. Can you say "Amen" to that?

May he make of us an eternal offering to you, so that we
may obtain an inheritance with our elect, especially with
the most Blessed Virgin Mary, Mother of God, with your
blessed Apostles and glorious Martyrs and with all the Saints,
on whose constant intercession in your presence we rely
for unfailing help.

Can you as a Protestant Christian say your "Amen" here?

May this Sacrifice of our reconciliation, we pray, O Lord,
advance the peace and salvation of all the world. Be pleased
to confirm in faith and charity your pilgrim Church on
earth, with your servant N. our Pope and N. our Bishop,
the Order of Bishops, all the clergy, and the entire people
you have gained for your own.

Can you say "Amen" to this? And can you join in the prayer
for the deceased? This is followed by the concluding words
of praise:

Through him, and with him, and in him, O God, almighty
Father, in the unity of the Holy Spirit, all glory and honor
is yours, for ever and ever.

To worthily receive Holy Communion, one must answer
"Amen" with the entire community to the eucharistic prayer
as a whole and to its individual parts to share essentially the
faith in which we then receive Holy Communion.

This is the simple "rule of thumb" that will allow Christians of other confessions to examine honestly whether they

can go to Communion in the Catholic Mass. Let me at once ward off a possible misunderstanding: this does not mean that we Catholics want to go fishing for Protestant Christians, so to speak, or to claim that they are "really" Catholics; all I want is to ask what the consequences are for ecclesial fellowship of the fact that a Protestant Christian can say this "Amen." How is one who says this "Amen" related to the fellowship of the Catholic Church?

These considerations have led me to formulate a request to Protestant Christians, which I have discussed with their Church leaders. If we wish to be honest and truthful in our dealings with one another, even on these difficult questions, we must encourage the members of our churches to do what their own church teaches and practices. We must not exhort Christians of other confessions to break with the praxis of their own confession.

For us Catholics, this means that since the Orthodox do not allow us to receive Communion in their liturgy, we respect this and do not receive Holy Communion there—although from our own point of view, this would in principle be possible.

My request to Protestant Christians is: Do not encourage us to break the rules of our Church—even if you do not understand why we should have such rules!

I believe that we can be extremely close to one another in this attitude of mutual reverence and respect, an attitude that respects these boundaries, because these boundaries *connect* us. We all have Christ, and what is more important or greater than fellowship with him and in him? This is the incomparably great gift he has given us through the Eucharist. And this is why we are entitled to hope and long for the day when we are all one in this gift.

INDEX OF BIBLICAL PASSAGES

SUBJECT INDEX